THE REIGN OF CLEOPATRA

Stanley M. Burstein

UNIVERSITY OF OKLAHOMA PRESS
Norman

To the memory of
Dr. Miriam Lichtheim (1914–2004),
distinguished Egyptologist and teacher.

Library of Congress Cataloging-in-Publication Data

Burstein, Stanley Mayer.
   The reign of Cleopatra / by Stanley M. Burstein.
     p.   cm.—(Greenwood guides to historic events of the ancient world)
   Includes bibliographical references and index.
   ISBN 978–0–8061–3871–8
   1. Cleopatra, Queen of Egypt, d. 30 B.C.   2. Egypt—History—332–30 B.C.
   3. Queens—Egypt—Biography. I. Title. II. Series.
DT92.7.B87   2004
932'.021'092—dc22   2004014672

British Library Cataloguing in Publication Data is available.

Library of Congress Catalog Card Number: 2004014672

The paper in this book meets the guidelines for permanence and durability of the Committee on Production Guidelines for Book Longevity of the Council on Library Sources, Inc. ∞

The Reign of Cleopatra, by Stanley M. Burstein, was originally published in hard cover by Greenwood Press, an imprint of Greenwood Publishing Group, Inc., Westport, CT. Copyright © 2004 by Stanley M. Burstein. First paperback edition published by the University of Oklahoma Press, Publishing Division of the University, 2007, by arrangement with Greenwood Publishing Group, Inc. All rights reserved. Manufactured in the United States of America.

1 2 3 4 5 6 7 8 9 10

CONTENTS

Photo essay follows Chapter 6.

PREFACE

Cleopatra VII is one of the most remarkable figures in ancient history. The last of the Ptolemaic rulers of Egypt, she struggled for two decades to preserve the independence of her kingdom and to restore the glory of her ancestors. Cleopatra's dramatic life was intertwined with those of some of the most powerful Romans of her time, including Julius Caesar, Mark Antony, and the future emperor Augustus. Her death in 30 B.C.E. brought to an end the history both of Egypt as an independent kingdom and of the successors of Alexander the Great. It also opened a two-millennia-long history of the queen as a potent symbol of female sexuality and power. Moreover, recent developments in the historiography of Ptolemaic Egypt make it possible for the first time to tell the story of Cleopatra's reign as a part of Egyptian history.[1]

The beginnings of the study of Ptolemaic Egypt date back to the early days of European imperial interest in modern Egypt in the nineteenth century. For much of the next century and a half historians reconstructed the history of Cleopatra's ancestors as a morality tale in which a foreign Greek dynasty gradually degenerated under the influence of the corrupting "orient," an object lesson for the new European masters of the Near East. Not surprisingly, fundamental changes in the historiography of Ptolemaic Egypt followed the disintegration of the European empires in Africa and the Near East after World War II.

By the 1970s scholars had recognized that Ptolemaic Egypt was better viewed as a distinct cultural entity with its own peculiar characteristics than subsumed in a hypothetical Greco-Roman Egypt. A decade later, social and cultural questions began to supplant the political and administrative concerns that had dominated the study of Ptolemaic Egypt since

the nineteenth century. The initial result was a new vision of social relations in Ptolemaic Egypt in which virtually separate Greek and Egyptian
societies and cultures tensely co-existed in Egypt with little or no interaction. Ethnicity was destiny, and the ethnicities that determined privilege
were Macedonian and Greek.

Evidence was not lacking to support this interpretation: obvious examples are prejudicial remarks about Egyptians in the sources, texts such as
The Potter's Oracle emphasizing tension between Greeks and Egyptians,
and repeated native rebellions. Nevertheless, increasing doubts about the
adequacy of this interpretation as a satisfactory description of Ptolemaic
Egyptian society have arisen during the past two decades. The problems
are threefold: first, it is based primarily on Greek textual evidence, which
tends to ignore non-Greeks; second, it exaggerates barriers to contact
between Greeks and non-Greeks in Ptolemaic Egypt; and third, like many
studies of modern colonial societies, it exaggerates the extent of ethnic
solidarity within the Egyptian population itself.

Part of the problem, of course, is that substantial social isolation characterized the one portion of the Egyptian population that is most visible
in the Greek sources, the rural poor. Study of the social life of Egyptian
cities and the use of Egyptian sources, however, have led scholars to
develop a more nuanced interpretation. Egyptian cities such as the ancient
Pharaonic capital Memphis turn out to have had a complex society in
which immigrant Greeks and native Egyptians lived side by side and inter-
acted closely. Similarly, study of the lives of the Egyptian elite has revealed
that native priests not only prospered in Ptolemaic Egypt but, far from
opposing the Ptolemies, were among the regime's strongest supporters. And
not only the elite. Even lower-level Egyptian officials such as royal scribes
prospered by exploiting their possession of a critical skill, Greco-Egyptian
bilingualism, to transform their "humble" office into one of considerable
power and influence.

This new view of life in Ptolemaic Egypt is not limited to the public
sphere. Close analysis of business and legal documents preserved by the
dry climate of Egypt revealed that Greek women living in Ptolemaic
Egypt exploited Egyptian law for their own economic advantage. It is not
surprising, therefore, that scholars increasingly view ethnicity in Ptolemaic Egypt as "situational," with individuals identifying themselves as
Egyptians or Greeks depending on the circumstances and advantages to
be gained, or that Egyptologists view the Hellenistic period as one of the

most innovative and creative periods in Egyptian literature, marked by significant achievements in traditional literary forms such as the tale and the appearance of new genres such as prose epic. As a result, it is possible for the first time to see Cleopatra in her proper historical context as the intelligent and able ruler of a multicultural Egypt. This book is a progress report on achieving that goal.

Chapter 1 provides a brief history of Ptolemaic rule in Egypt, from the conquest of Alexander the Great in 332 B.C.E. to the accession of Cleopatra's father Ptolemy XII in 80 B.C.E. The chapter traces the expansion of Ptolemaic power in the eastern Mediterranean basin in the third century B.C.E. and its gradual decline in the second century B.C.E. It also describes the gradual transformation of Rome from a distant but benevolent power to a major threat to Egyptian independence.

Having described the historical context of Cleopatra's reign, Chapter 2 recounts her life. The chapter describes her gradual emergence as ruler of Egypt and her efforts to preserve the independence of her kingdom by enlisting the support of Julius Caesar and Mark Antony. It also makes clear that Cleopatra was not simply a "sexual predator" but an able queen with realistic and potentially achievable goals.

Although the narrative of Cleopatra's reign necessarily focuses on her relations with Rome and Romans, the reality was that governing Egypt occupied the bulk of her life. The next three chapters deal with that reality. Chapter 3 discusses the organization of Egypt and how the discovery of ancient papyri has enabled scholars to reconstruct how the government of Cleopatra's Egypt worked. Chapter 4 analyzes the complex society of Ptolemaic Egypt, exploring the interaction of Egyptians, Greeks, and Jews in one of the earliest known multicultural societies. Chapter 5 focuses on Alexandria—Cleopatra's capital—and its remarkable culture, which made it the principal city of the Hellenistic world. Finally, the conclusion traces the long and complex afterlife of Cleopatra as a symbol in Western culture.

The book also includes sections containing brief biographies of sixteen figures who played major roles in Cleopatra's life, as well as a selection of the principal primary sources documenting the history of her reign. The biographies will give substance to the figures only briefy mentioned in the text, while the documents will provide readers with examples of the evidence used to reconstruct her biography. A glossary of selected terms, an appendix on the Ptolemies, and an annotated bibliography conclude the book.

In the course of the preparation of *The Reign of Cleopatra* I incurred many debts. I would particularly like to thank Professor Erich Gruen of the University of California at Berkeley, who kindly provided me with a copy of his article "Cleopatra in Rome: Facts and Fantasies" prior to its publication. I would also like to express my gratitude to Professors Brendan Nagle of the University of Southern California and Miriam E. Burstein of the State University of New York at Brockport for reading and commenting on earlier versions of the manuscript, and Professor Bella Vivante of the University of Arizona, for inviting me to write this book and for her constant support and encouragement.

CHRONOLOGY OF EVENTS

332 B.C.E.	Alexander the Great conquers Egypt and establishes Macedonian rule. He also founds the city of Alexandria.
323–283 B.C.E.	Ptolemy, son of Lagos, receives Egypt as his satrapy in the division of Alexander's empire in the summer of 323 B.C.E. During his forty-year reign, he creates an Egyptian empire by annexing Libya, Cyprus, and Koile Syria. He also founds the Museum and Library.
283–246 B.C.E.	Ptolemy II succeeds his father as king. During his thirty-seven-year reign, he defends the Egyptian empire against Seleucid attacks, while expanding Ptolemaic power in Nubia, the Aegean, and Anatolia. He completes building the Pharos lighthouse and the Museum and Library. He also organizes the administration of Egypt and establishes the cult of the ruler and the practice of royal incest by marrying his sister, Arsinoe II.
273 B.C.E.	Ptolemy II opens relations with Rome by sending an embassy to congratulate Rome for its victory in its war with Pyrrhos, king of Epiros.
245 B.C.E.	Ptolemy III invades Syria and Mesopotamia, and expands the Ptolemaic empire to its greatest extent.

217 B.C.E.	Ptolemy IV defeats the Seleukid king Antiochos III in the Battle of Raphia, preserving Ptolemaic rule in Koile Syria.
207 B.C.E.	Rebellion breaks out in Upper Egypt supported by native troops armed by Ptolemy IV for the Battle of Raphia and the kingdom of Kush in Nubia. For two decades the Ptolemies lose control of southern Egypt to two native Egyptian kings, Herwennefer and Ankhwennefer.
200 B.C.E.	Ptolemy V's government seeks Roman support against the agreement between Antiochos III and Philip V of Macedon to divide up Ptolemaic foreign possessions. Rome orders both not to attack Ptolemaic territory.
197 B.C.E.	Antiochos III defeats the forces of Ptolemy V at the Battle of Panion and occupies Koile Syria and Anatolia, beginning the dismemberment of the Ptolemaic empire.
194 B.C.E.	Ptolemy V marries Cleopatra I, daughter of Antiochos III, without informing Rome. Relations with Rome deteriorate as a result.
186 B.C.E.	Ptolemy V defeats Ankhwennefer and his Kushite allies and reunites Egypt.
168 B.C.E.	Rome defeats Macedon in the Third Macedonian War and suppresses the Macedonian monarchy. A Roman ambassador orders Antiochos IV to withdraw from Egypt, frustrating his plan to unite Egypt and Syria.
163 B.C.E.	Ptolemy VI agrees to his brother's ruling an independent kingdom in Libya in order to end Ptolemy VIII's efforts to supplant him as king of Egypt. Ptolemy VIII tries to induce the Roman Senate to force his brother to give him Cyprus.

156/5 B.C.E.	Ptolemy VIII draws up a will leaving his kingdom to Rome following an unsuccessful assassination attempt on his life.
145–116 B.C.E.	Ptolemy VIII becomes king of Egypt and reunites the Egyptian empire.
c. 106 B.C.E.	Ptolemy IX Soter II rules Cyprus as an independent kingdom.
c. 100 B.C.E.	Ptolemy XII is born to Ptolemy XI and an unknown woman.
96 B.C.E.	Ptolemy Apion—king of Libya and son of Ptolemy VIII—dies, leaving Libya to Rome in his will.
88 B.C.E.	Ptolemy X dies, leaving Egypt and Cyprus to Rome in his will.
80 B.C.E.	The Greek citizens of Alexandria murder Ptolemy XI and divide the remaining territories of the Ptolemies, making Ptolemy XII king of Egypt and his brother Ptolemy king of Cyprus.
70s B.C.E.	Ptolemy XII marries his sister, Cleopatra V Tryphaina, who bears him a daughter, Berenike. He probably also forms a relationship with an unknown Egyptian woman.
74 B.C.E.	Rome accepts the legacy of Ptolemy Apion and organizes Libya as a province.
70 B.C.E.	Cleopatra VII is born, the second daughter of Ptolemy XII.
60s B.C.E.	Arsinoe IV is born.
67–63 B.C.E.	Pompey defeats Mithridates VI of Pontus and conquers Syria and Palestine.
63 B.C.E.	Roman tribune unsuccessfully proposes to annex Egypt. Pompey suppresses the Jewish monarchy in Judaea. Ptolemy XII offers assistance to him.

61 B.C.E.	Ptolemy XIII is born.
59 B.C.E.	Ptolemy XII is recognized as king of Egypt and friend of the Roman people through a law moved by Julius Caesar at the cost of huge bribes. Ptolemy XIV is born.
58 B.C.E.	Rome acts on the will of Ptolemy X and annexes Cyprus. Ptolemy of Cyprus commits suicide. Ptolemy XII is exiled by the Alexandrians, who make his eldest daughter, Berenike, and his wife, Cleopatra V, joint rulers.
57 B.C.E.	Cleopatra V dies, leaving Berenike as sole ruler of Egypt. Ptolemy XII seeks help in Rome to restore himself to power.
55 B.C.E.	Aulus Gabinius, governor of Syria, returns Ptolemy XII to power, who executes his daughter Berenike and purges his enemies in Alexandria.
54 B.C.E.	Rome launches an unsuccessful invasion of Parthia. Marcus Crass is defeated and killed in the Battle of Carrhae in Syria.
52 B.C.E.	Cleopatra VII becomes Ptolemy XII's co-regent as ruler of Egypt.
51 B.C.E.	Ptolemy XII dies, leaving a will in which he makes his eldest son, Ptolemy XIII, and Cleopatra VII joint rulers and the Roman people their guardians. Before his death, he sends the will to Rome where it is received and kept by Pompey. Ptolemy XIII marries Cleopatra.
50 B.C.E.	Cleopatra suppresses her brother and rules Egypt alone for most of the year. Ptolemy XIII returns to power, exiling Cleopatra.
49/8 B.C.E.	Cleopatra gathers an army in Syria and attempts to regain power.

48 B.C.E.	After his defeat in the Battle of Pharsalus, Pompey flees to Egypt, where he is murdered by agents of Ptolemy XIII. Julius Caesar comes to Alexandria. He reconciles Ptolemy XIII and Cleopatra VII and returns Cyprus to Ptolemaic rule. Caesar and Cleopatra are besieged in Alexandria by the forces of Ptolemy XIII and his sister Arsinoe. Ptolemy XIII is killed in battle and Arsinoe is captured. Cleopatra VII becomes queen of Egypt as the wife of Ptolemy XIV.
47 B.C.E.	Cleopatra gives birth to a son by Caesar whom she names Ptolemy Caesarion.
46 B.C.E.	Cleopatra, Ptolemy XIV, and Caesarion visit Rome for the first time. Cleopatra is recognized as a friend of the Roman people. Caesar holds a triumph for his victories in Gaul, Egypt, Pontus, and Mauretania. Caesar orders Cleopatra's sister Arsinoe to go into exile at Ephesus.
44 B.C.E.	Cleopatra visits Rome for the second time with Caesarion and Ptolemy XIV. Julius Caesar is assassinated on March 15. Cleopatra returns to Egypt. Ptolemy XIV dies under mysterious circumstances and Caesarion is crowned king as Ptolemy Caesar-ion.
43 B.C.E.	Civil war breaks out at Rome. Octavian, Mark Antony, and Marcus Lepidus form the Second Triumvirate to fight the senatorial forces led by Caesar's assassins Brutus and Cassius.
42 B.C.E.	The forces of Brutus and Cassius are defeated in the Battle of Philippi by the triumviral army commanded by Antony.
41 B.C.E.	Cleopatra is summoned to meet Antony at Tarsus to explain her actions during the civil war. Cleopatra is pardoned and her control of Egypt is recognized. Arsinoe is executed at Ephesus on orders of

Antony in accordance with his agreement with Cleopatra.

40 B.C.E.

Antony spends the winter in Alexandria as the guest of Cleopatra. Antony returns to Italy and comes to terms with Octavian. Their renewed alliance is sealed by Antony's marriage to Octavian's sister Octavia. Cleopatra bears her first children by Antony, the twins Alexander Helios and Cleopatra Selene.

37 B.C.E.

After a three-year absence, Antony returns to Antioch in Syria to make plans for a major campaign against Parthia. Cleopatra meets Antony in Antioch, where he transfers to Egyptian rule Cyprus, Crete, Kyrene, several cities in Phoenicia, Syria, Cilicia, and the Arab kingdom of Iturea in northern Palestine. Antony recognizes Alexander Helios and Cleopatra Selene as his children.

36 B.C.E.

Cleopatra gives birth to Ptolemy Philadelphos, her last child by Antony. Antony's Parthian Campaign ends in complete failure. After the return of his army to Syria, Antony goes to Egypt with Cleopatra.

34 B.C.E.

Antony invades Armenia, captures the king of Armenia, and makes Armenia a Roman province. Antony and Cleopatra celebrate his victory over the king of Armenia, concluding with the recognition of Caesarion as the son of Julius Caesar and the assignment of territories within and without the Roman Empire to Cleopatra and their children.

33–32 B.C.E.

Relations between Antony and Octavian deteriorate openly. Antony divorces Octavia and marries Cleopatra. Octavian persuades the Senate to declare war on Cleopatra instead of Antony.

31 B.C.E.

Warfare breaks out between Antony and Octavian, concluding with the defeat of Antony and Cleopatra's forces in the Battle of Actium. Antony and Cleopatra escape to Egypt, while the remainder of Antony's navy and army in Greece surrender to Octavian.

30 B.C.E.   Octavian conquers Egypt. Antony and Cleopatra commit suicide. Octavian executes Caesarion, and reorganizes Egypt as Roman territory.

29 B.C.E.   Octavian returns to Rome with the surviving children of Cleopatra. He celebrates his triumph over Cleopatra in which for the first time the idea that she died of a snake bite appears.

20s B.C.E.   Alexander Helios and Ptolemy Philadelphos die.

c. 25–19 B.C.E.   Cleopatra Selene marries Juba II of Mauretania.

c. 5 B.C.E.   Cleopatra Selene dies.

c. 23/24 C.E.   Ptolemy, the son of Juba II and Cleopatra Selene, becomes king of Mauretania.

c. 37–41 C.E.   Ptolemy of Mauretania is executed by the emperor Caligula, ending the family of Ptolemy I.

CHAPTER 1

HISTORICAL
BACKGROUND

The dramatic reign of Cleopatra VII closed one of the most brilliant periods in ancient Egyptian history. For almost three centuries her ancestors ruled Egypt and extended Egyptian influence throughout the Aegean and western Asia and deep into Africa and Arabia. Not for over a thousand years had Egyptian power and influence been felt over so wide an area. This final period of Egyptian greatness was made possible by one of the decisive events of ancient history: the conquest of the Persian Empire by Alexander III of Macedon in the late fourth century B.C.E.

Alexander's extraordinary conquests mark the beginning of a new epoch in the history of the ancient world that historians call the Hellenistic period. The Hellenistic period extends from the accession of Alexander as king of Macedon in 336 B.C.E. to the Roman conquest of Egypt in 30 B.C.E. The term *Hellenistic* means "Greek-like," and was originally used to stigmatize the visual arts and literature of the period after Alexander as a decline from the purity and simplicity that characterized works of the classical period. Contemporary historians, however, have a more positive view of the Hellenistic period, seeing these three centuries as a time in which Greeks and Greek culture enjoyed unprecedented prestige in western Asia and the eastern Mediterranean. Far from being inferior to the achievements of classical Greece, the works of Hellenistic artists, writers, scientists, and philosophers were of vital importance to the formation of later Western and Islamic culture. The origins of the Hellenistic world in all its remarkable variety and richness lay in the kingdom of Macedon.

PTOLEMY I AND THE FOUNDATION OF THE PTOLEMAIC DYNASTY

Macedon had been a minor Balkan kingdom until the mid–fourth century B.C.E., when Alexander's father Philip II transformed it into the strongest military power in the eastern Mediterranean. In just over two decades, he subdued the Balkans from the Danube River to southern Greece and organized the various city-states and ethnic confederations of Greece into an alliance known as the Korinthian League, which had as its purpose the maintenance of Macedonian authority in Greece and the invasion of the Persian Empire. Although Macedonian forces were already campaigning in the Anatolian provinces of the Persian Empire in early 336 B.C.E., Philip's ultimate goals remain unknown, since his dramatic assassination in the summer of 336 B.C.E. during his daughter's wedding not only aborted his plans but also threatened to undo all that he had accomplished in the Balkans.

The accession of his twenty-year-old son Alexander III saved Philip's hard-won empire, averting civil war in Macedon and rebellion by its Balkan and Greek subjects. Alexander did far more, however, than merely survive. During his thirteen-year reign, he carried out one of the most remarkable military campaigns in world history, leading his army all the way to western India and unexpectedly fulfilling the seemingly impossible dream of Greek intellectuals of conquering the mighty Persian Empire, which had ruled western Asia for over two centuries.

Alexander's conquests made possible a new social and political order in western Asia and the eastern Mediterranean, but he would not be responsible for determining its shape or character. His unexpected death at Babylon in the summer of 323 B.C.E. at the age of thirty-three aborted any plans he may have had for a new political organization for his vast empire, leaving the destruction of the Persian Empire as his primary achievement. It would fall to his successors to determine the nature of his legacy. Four decades of bitter civil war between Alexander's generals followed Alexander's death before a new order emerged in the former territories of the Persian Empire.

The principal casualty of these wars was Alexander's dynasty, which fell victim to the ambitions of his generals and the dream of maintaining the unity of the empire. For almost two decades Antigonos the One-Eyed, one of the last surviving commanders of Philip II, struggled to hold the empire together against the bitter opposition of his rivals, finally dying in battle at the age of eighty in 301 B.C.E. When the dust cleared two decades later in 281 B.C.E., the last traces of Alexander's great empire had disappeared. In its place was a series of kingdoms ruled by Macedonian dynasties scattered throughout the territories of the old Persian Empire. Three of these new kingdoms were of particular importance: Macedon, which was ruled by the descendants of Antigonos the One-Eyed; the kingdom of Syria, which controlled the central provinces of the old Persian Empire and was ruled by Seleukos I; and the kingdom of Egypt, which was controlled by Cleopatra's great ancestor, Ptolemy I.

Ptolemy I's first contact with Egypt occurred in 332 B.C.E., when the Persians surrendered it to Alexander without a fight. The full extent of his activities during the short time Alexander stayed in Egypt is unknown. As one of the king's oldest friends and a member of his personal entourage, however, he was certainly present when Alexander laid the foundations for Alexandria—the future capital of Ptolemaic Egypt—and he probably shared the king's daring and dangerous visit to the oasis of Siwah, where the oracle revealed that Alexander was the son of the Egyptian god Amon.

Whatever the details of Ptolemy I's initial encounter with Egypt, he was clearly impressed by the country's great wealth and potential, as is evident from his actions during the succession crisis that broke out after Alexander unexpectedly died without leaving any obvious heir. During the ensuing crisis, Ptolemy opposed the maintenance of strong royal authority, favoring instead the establishment of a weak regency council dominated by Alexander's principal commanders while the empire itself was divided among the regents and their colleagues.

Ptolemy's separatist approach to the empire found no followers in the immediate aftermath of Alexander's death. Instead, a strong regent was appointed for Alexander's joint successors—his mentally retarded half brother Philip III and the infant Alexander IV—in the person of Perdikkas, the commander of the Macedonian cavalry and the head of the imperial administration. Ptolemy did, however, receive Egypt as his satrapy in the division of Alexander's empire, which closed the first phase of the struggle over the fate of the empire.

Throughout the forty years of his reign (323 B.C.E.–283 B.C.E.), Ptolemy I worked diligently to give legitimacy to his rule of Egypt and to ensure its security by creating buffers on its principal frontiers. His first step was to secure Egypt's western frontier by converting the city of Kyrene in Libya into a protectorate governed by a Ptolemaic official. Ptolemy I's Kyrenean adventure aroused no resistance from his potential rivals among Alexander's other generals; not so for his next move: the diversion of Alexander's funeral cortege to Egypt in 321 B.C.E. as it was transporting Alexander's body to Macedon for burial. At a time when all Macedonian rulers derived their ultimate legitimacy from their personal contact with Alexander, possession of Alexander's body gave Ptolemy I and his successors unique prestige. It is not surprising, therefore, that he had to fight to retain his prize, thwarting in 321 B.C.E. an attempted invasion of Egypt by the outraged regent Perdikkas by breaching the Nile canals and drowning much of Perdikkas's army, or that Alexander's tomb in Alexandria became the central shrine of his dynasty.

Victory over Perdikkas legitimized Ptolemy I's control of Egypt. Ptolemy I henceforth considered Egypt as spear-won land and, therefore, his by right of conquest—independent of any decision by Philip III and Alexander IV or their future regent. At the same time, his rejection of the regency after the assassination of Perdikkas reflected his continuing belief that division of the empire into separate kingdoms was both inevitable and desirable.

For the next two decades, Ptolemy I joined with Seleukos, Kassander—the successor of Alexander's dynasty as ruler of Macedon—and Lysimachos—the satrap of Thrace—to oppose Antigonos the One-Eyed's attempt to restore the empire. Like his allies, Ptolemy asserted his independence by quickly proclaiming himself king in response to Antigonos the One-Eyed's proclamation of his own kingship in 305 B.C.E. At the same time, however, he also carefully avoided direct involvement in the great military campaign of 302/1 B.C.E. that put an end to Antigonos's imperial dreams.

Although Ptolemy I did not take part in the decisive campaign against Antigonos, he did profit from it, taking advantage of Seleukos's absence to add the remainder of Koile Syria (hollow Syria)—essentially modern Israel, Jordan, Lebanon, and southern Syria—to Judaea, which he had conquered in 307 B.C.E., allegedly by taking advantage of Jews' obligation of resting on the Sabbath to occupy Jerusalem. Less than a decade later, Ptolemy I rounded out his empire by annexing Cyprus, which gave him important naval bases from which Egyptian power could be projected into the eastern Mediterranean and Aegean Seas.

It had been more than three hundred years since the power of an Egyptian king had extended over so much of the territory of Egypt's neighbors. Not only had Ptolemy I accomplished his goal of building a strong buffer around Egypt, but he had also greatly increased Egypt's wealth. The conquest of Cyprus and Koile Syria gave Egypt access to important mineral and timber resources, while control of the ports of Koile Syria (such as Gaza) enabled Ptolemy I and his successors to tap directly into important trade routes from Mesopotamia and the incense-producing regions of southern Arabia that led to them.

Ptolemy I's success, however, contained the seeds of his dynasty's eventual decline. The problem was Koile Syria; Seleukos considered it his because of his role in the defeat of Antigonos the One-Eyed and believed that Ptolemy I had robbed him of his prize. Regaining Koile Syria would obsess his successors throughout the third century B.C.E. Ptolemy I countered Seleukos' hostility by forming alliances with Lysimachos and important Greek cities such as Athens, but it would fall to Ptolemy II Philadelphos and his successors to cope with the fallout from Ptolemy I's achievements.

THE PEAK OF PTOLEMAIC POWER: PTOLEMY II (282–245 B.C.E.) AND PTOLEMY III (245–222 B.C.E.)

Ptolemy II Philadelphos (Sibling Loving God) is best known for his unprecedented and controversial marriage to his full sister Arsinoe II. Although Ptolemy II's reasons for entering into this unconventional union are unknown, Arsinoe proved to be a capable and popular partner, and their marriage set a precedent for many of his successors, including Cleopatra VII. Emphasis on his marriage, however, can easily obscure the significant achievements of Ptolemy II's reign. Domestically, he systematized the complex administrative system that ran Ptolemaic Egypt, and completed many of the projects Ptolemy I had begun, including the great Pharos lighthouse and the Museum and Library in Alexandria. Foreign affairs, however, dominated his reign.

While Seleukos I had not pressed his claim to Koile Syria militarily, his successors Antiochos I and Antiochos II did so repeatedly. As a result, Ptolemy II fought three wars with the Seleukids during his long reign. His goals were to maintain his father's legacy and to keep hostilities away from Egypt. To that end, Ptolemy II rarely confronted Seleukid forces directly. Instead, he exploited his dynasty's superior naval forces to wage war around the western periphery of the Seleukid Empire. At the same time, he used the enormous wealth and prestige of Egypt to prevent the Seleukid's Macedonian allies from intervening in the fighting by encouraging major Greek cities such as Athens and Sparta to reassert their independence in the so-called Chremonidean War (c. 268–262 B.C.E.). The result of this long struggle was a stalemate that left Ptolemy II firmly in control of the core of his empire: Cyprus, Koile Syria, and Kyrene.

The Ptolemies were also well positioned to exploit any hint of Seleukid weakness. Such an opportunity occurred shortly after the death of Ptolemy II in 245 B.C.E., when Berenike—his daughter and widow of Antiochos II—invited his successor, Ptolemy III Euergetes (benefactor), to intervene on behalf of her child in the succession crisis that had erupted in the Seleukid empire. Although Ptolemy III was unable to save his sister and nephew, his army campaigned throughout much of the Seleukid empire, reaching as far as the borders of Iran before returning to Egypt, laden with booty and glory.

The results of Ptolemy III's spectacular campaign were substantial. Although Ptolemy III exaggerated by portraying himself to his Greek and Egyptian subjects as a conqueror comparable to Alexander the Great, he was able to exploit his success to strengthen significantly Ptolemaic power in Anatolia and the northern Aegean. Meanwhile, the Seleukid empire fell into chaos. In the west, the sons of Antiochos II fought bitterly over the succession to the throne while the Parthians, an Iranian people from central Asia and the future conquerors of the Seleukid state, took advantage of the chaos to settle in western Iran. At about the same time, the satrap of Baktria—modern Afghanistan—asserted his independence, founding a Greek-dominated kingdom that would exert a powerful influence on political and cultural events in central Asia and northern India.

The long confrontation with the Seleukids also led to a major expansion of Ptolemaic activity in Nubia and the Red Sea basin. Although Egyptian involvement in Nubia can be traced to the earliest days of pharaonic history and Ptolemy I even briefly campaigned in Nubia, it was only during the reign of Ptolemy II that large-scale Ptolemaic activity in the region began. The reasons for the involvement were twofold: first, they needed to counter the claims to Lower Nubia of the kingdom of

Kush, based near the fourth cataract of the Nile at the city of Napata; and second, and more important, they needed to acquire access to a secure source of elephants.

The use of war elephants was long established in Asia, and the beasts had gained a fearsome reputation during the campaigns of Alexander and the first generation of his successors. Since geography and good relations with the Maurya rulers of north India gave the Seleukids privileged access to Indian elephants, Ptolemy II and Ptolemy III looked to Nubia to offset the Seleukid advantage in elephants. A war fought between Ptolemy II and Kush in the 270s B.C.E. gave Ptolemy II control of the important gold-mining region immediately south of Egypt known as the Dodekaskoinos and free access to Kushite territory farther south. As a result, he and his successor, Ptolemy III, built an extensive series of hunting stations and ports as far south as modern Port Sudan in central Sudan from which Ptolemaic hunting parties—sometimes numbering hundreds of men—roamed freely through the eastern Sudan, seeking elephants for capture and transport to Egypt and for their ivory.

Large-scale Ptolemaic elephant hunting in Nubia lasted for almost three quarters of a century and produced important results. Most obvious were the development of a corps of war elephants that could confront Seleukid elephants in battle, and a greatly improved knowledge of the geography and ethnography of Nubia and the Red Sea basin. Less obvious but equally important was the growth of Ptolemaic influence in the kingdom of Kush. A Greek-educated Nubian king named Ergamenes (Arqamani) overthrew Kush's priestly elite, which had played a major role in the kingdom's governance since its foundation in the eighth century B.C.E., thereby opening the way for increased trade with Egypt and a substantial expansion of Ptolemaic Egyptian and Greek cultural influence in Nubia.

Ptolemaic diplomatic and commercial activity was not, however, limited to Nubia. Sea trade also began in the third century B.C.E. with the wealthy incense-bearing kingdoms of Yemen and southern Arabia. Ptolemy II even sent an ambassador to India, possibly providing the occasion for the Buddhist Indian emperor Asoka to send a counterembassy to Egypt to preach Buddhism there. Unfortunately, nothing is known of the results of Asoka's Buddhist embassy, not even if it actually reached Egypt.

THE DECLINE OF PTOLEMAIC POWER: FROM PTOLEMY IV PHILOPATOR TO PTOLEMY XII NEOS DIONYSOS (222 B.C.E.–80 B.C.E.)

The preeminence of Ptolemaic Egypt among the Hellenistic kingdoms lasted for a little over two decades. Its decline began during the reign of Ptolemy III's successor, Ptolemy IV Philopator (222 B.C.E.–204 B.C.E.). Ironically, Ptolemy IV began his reign by inflicting on the young Seleukid king Antiochos III a defeat almost as severe as that of 245 B.C.E. Obsessed like his predecessors by the determination to reassert Seleukid power over Koile Syria, Antiochos III launched an invasion in 219 B.C.E. that brought him control of most of the area, only to lose it all in 217 B.C.E., when he suffered a crushing defeat at the hands of Ptolemy IV at Raphia, in present-day Israel.

The Battle of Raphia was the last great Ptolemaic military victory over the Seleukids. The subsequent fate of the two monarchs involved in the battle, however, differed dramatically. Antiochos III worked diligently to reconstitute his forces in the years after the battle. By 212 B.C.E., Antiochos III's position was secure enough that he could undertake a seven-year campaign that would repeat Alexander's march and restore Seleukid authority throughout much of the vast area between Mesopotamia and the borders of India, and gain Antiochos III a formidable reputation as a conquering king in the mold of his great ancestors. Meanwhile, Ptolemaic rule in Egypt disintegrated. Ptolemy IV had recruited large numbers of Egyptian soldiers for the Battle of Raphia, and soon after the battle, they became the nucleus for native revolts throughout Upper Egypt. At the time of his death in 204 B.C.E., Ptolemy IV had lost control of Upper Egypt to native pharaohs supported by Kush, who would rule it until they were finally suppressed by his successor Ptolemy V Epiphanes (the manifest god) in 186 B.C.E.

The crisis came at the end of the third century B.C.E. With Ptolemy V still a child and his government locked in a struggle for survival with native pharaohs in Upper Egypt, the far-flung Ptolemaic empire was vulnerable. Antiochos III and Philip V of Macedon entered into a secret agreement in 202 B.C.E. to divide up the Ptolemies' foreign possessions. Within a year, most Ptolemaic possessions in the north Aegean and southern Anatolia had fallen to the kings.

Although the agreement was secret, news of it leaked out, resulting in Ptolemy V's regents together with other states appealing to Rome, the only power strong enough to confront the joint forces of Antiochos III and Philip V. The appeal to Rome was understandable. Rome had just defeated the North African city-state of Carthage in the Second Punic War, making it the dominant power in the western Mediterranean. Moreover, relations between the Ptolemies and Rome had been good ever since Ptolemy II Philadelphos had sent an embassy to Rome in 273 B.C.E. to congratulate the Senate on its defeat of Pyrrhos, the king of Epirus. The Romans had been flattered and welcomed the recognition of the rich and powerful king of Egypt, and relations between the Ptolemies and the rising power in the west had remained cordial for the rest of the third century B.C.E. Ptolemaic friendship had, indeed, worked to Rome's advantage during the third century B.C.E., allowing the republic to fight Carthage without fear of Egyptian intervention.

The Ptolemaic government's hopes were fulfilled in that the Senate ordered the kings to abandon their designs on the Ptolemaic empire. Unfortunately, Rome then became bogged down in the Second Macedonian War (200–197 B.C.E.), leaving Antiochos III free to pursue his own goals with only Roman diplomacy to deter him. By 197 B.C.E., he had driven Ptolemaic forces from Koile Syria, then turned north and overran the remaining Ptolemaic possessions in Anatolia. Antiochos III had finally realized his ancestors' dream of regaining the territory "stolen" from Seleukos I by Ptolemy I a century earlier. Desperate to secure the safety of Egypt, Ptolemy V's regents made a separate peace with Antiochos III in 195 B.C.E., abandoning Ptolemaic claims to much of their former empire as part of a deal that united the two Macedonian royal houses through a marriage between the young Ptolemy V and Antiochos III's daughter Cleopatra I.

However understandable the decision to make peace with Antiochos III may have been, the fact that it had been made without consulting the Senate soured relations between Rome and Egypt, which became immediately apparent. Acting on the assumption that the separate peace between Ptolemy V and Antiochos III freed them of any responsibility to support Ptolemaic interests, the Senate ignored Ptolemaic claims to territories captured from Philip V in the Second Macedonian War, assigning them instead to Rome's chief allies in the war—the kingdom of

Pergamon in northwest Anatolia and the island state of Rhodes. Similarly, after defeating Antiochos III in 190 B.C.E., Rome allowed him and his dynasty to retain Koile Syria, leaving Ptolemy V with only Cyprus and Kyrene as the principal remaining territories of his dynasty's once vast empire. Worse, however, was to follow.

As Rome became ever more clearly the dominant power in the Mediterranean in the course of the second century B.C.E., its suspicions of all real or potential rivals grew, and it freely used its military and diplomatic power to undermine states it viewed as potential threats. Egypt was no exception. Although Rome did save Egypt from absorption into the Seleukid state in 168 B.C.E. by peremptorily ordering Antiochos IV Epiphanes to withdraw from Egypt or face war, the Senate repeatedly intervened in Egyptian affairs, forcing Ptolemy VI Philometor (mother-loving god) to recognize Kyrene as an independent kingdom ruled by his ambitious brother Ptolemy VIII Euergetes and unsuccessfully supporting a similar status for Cyprus.

As a ploy to strengthen his own position against his brother, Ptolemy VIII drew up a will naming Rome as his heir—a practice that would later be repeated. Although Roman pressure on Egypt eased during the long and turbulent reign of its protégé Ptolemy VIII (145–116 B.C.E.) despite his ruling Egypt, Kyrene, and Cyprus, it resumed after his death. By the end of the second century B.C.E., Kyrene was again a separate kingdom ruled by an illegitimate son of Ptolemy VIII's named Ptolemy Apion, who followed his father's example and named Rome his heir in his will.

By the early first century B.C.E., however, Rome's reluctance to annex territories in the eastern Mediterranean had long since disappeared. The Senate, therefore, readily accepted the bequest of Kyrene on learning of the death of Ptolemy Apion in 96 B.C.E., thereby gaining possession of the oldest portion of the Ptolemies' once great foreign empire. The organization of Kyrene as a Roman province two decades later in 75/4 B.C.E. brought Roman power almost to within sight of Alexandria. Not surprisingly, preventing Egypt from suffering the same fate would be the overriding goal of Ptolemy XII Neos Dionysos—the father of Cleopatra VII—from his accession to the throne in 80 B.C.E. to his death almost three decades later in 51 B.C.E.

CHAPTER 2

Cleopatra's Life

The Roman threat dominated Cleopatra's life just as it did her father's. Cleopatra VII was born in 69 B.C.E., the second of the five children of Ptolemy XII Neos Dionysos (the new Dionysos), who had ruled Egypt since the death of Ptolemy X Alexander II in 80 B.C.E. Cleopatra's mother is unknown. Historians have generally assumed that her mother was Ptolemy XII's sister and wife, Cleopatra V Tryphaina, but Cleopatra's contemporary, the geographer Strabo, noted that she and her younger siblings were illegitimate. There is strong circumstantial evidence pointing to her mother being an Egyptian, possibly a relative of the high priest of the temple of Ptah, the Egyptian creator god, at Memphis, who had crowned her father king and was the most important priest in Egypt.[1]

We know nothing about Cleopatra's childhood and teenage years. She suddenly emerges on the historical scene in 50 B.C.E. as a clear-headed, resourceful, and, above all, ambitious young queen fully able to match wits with her rivals and to engage the interest of Romans such as Julius Caesar. The source of her abilities must lie in these lost years.

THE LOST YEARS: 69–50 B.C.E.

Legend ascribes much of Cleopatra's success to her beauty and sexuality, but the ancient sources emphasize her intelligence and charm rather than her physical beauty, which they claim was average. She was reputed to understand eight languages and to be the first of her dynasty to speak Egyptian, the language of her subjects. She is supposed to have written books on a variety of subjects including weights and measures, cosmetics, and even magic. In the third and second centuries, major poets and scholars served as tutors to Ptolemaic princes and princesses. This was probably also true of Cleopatra and her siblings, especially since that was how she educated her own children, hiring the noted historian and philosopher Nikolaos of Damascus to tutor the twins she bore Mark Antony in 40 B.C.E. Her most important teacher, however, was undoubtedly her father, Ptolemy XII.

Ptolemy XII's obsession with retaining his throne at all costs, and his extravagant passion for Dionysos—the Greek god of wine and music, whom Greeks identified with the Egyptian royal god Osiris—including his practice of accompanying Dionysiac choruses on the flute, earned him the sobriquet Auletes (flute player) from his contemporaries and the scorn of historians since antiquity. The young Cleopatra probably understood little of the theology that underlay her father's religious views. She was, however, an astute observer of the spectacular religious pageantry of her father's court, with its sensuality and music, as her later masterful use of religious spectacle to advance her political goals makes clear. Ptolemy XII's most important contributions to her education, however, were the harsh lessons in practical politics she gained from observing his struggle to keep his throne in the face of ruthless Roman politicians and ambitious members of his own family.

Ptolemy XII's hold on the throne of Egypt was insecure from the moment of his accession in 80 B.C.E. Because he was the illegitimate son of Ptolemy IX, his right to rule was always open to challenge, especially by Roman politicians, who increasingly viewed Egypt as a rich prize ready for the taking and claimed that Egypt's last legitimate king, Ptolemy X Alexander II, had left the kingdom to Rome in his will should he die without heirs.

The danger posed by Ptolemy X's will first became palpable in 63 B.C.E., when Cleopatra was barely seven years old. A tribune named P. Servilius Rullus proposed that Rome annex Egypt as provided in the will of Ptolemy X and use its rich farmland as part of an agrarian reform scheme supposedly intended to provide land for the Roman poor.

Fortunately for Ptolemy XII, Rullus' legislation failed. Roman politics in the middle and late 60s B.C.E. was dominated by fear of Pompey, who had finally overthrown Mithridates VI of Pontus and was building an enormous reputation and personal following as he campaigned successfully throughout the Near East. Although Rullus' agrarian law purportedly was intended to aid the Roman people, its real purpose had been to hobble Pompey by providing a great military command for his rivals Marcus Licinius Crassus and Gaius Julius Caesar.

Ptolemy XII meanwhile sought to gain the support of Pompey, sending him a valuable gold crown in 63 B.C.E. and promising to pay for a force of eight thousand cavalry, ostensibly to assist in the conquest of Judaea. He also invited Pompey to come to Egypt and restore order. While Pompey rejected Ptolemy's tempting invitation, he did accept the crown and the cavalry troopers, thereby establishing a tie with the Egyptian monarch that would last until the end of his reign.

Four years later, Ptolemy XII's investment must have seemed worth the high cost. Pompey, Crassus, and Julius Caesar formed the First Triumvirate in 60 B.C.E., and one of their first acts was to recognize Ptolemy XII as king of Egypt and ally of Rome. But Ptolemy XII's joy was short-lived. Caesar's demands for supporting Ptolemy's claim to the throne had exceeded the king's resources, forcing him to borrow more than six thousand talents from Roman moneylenders. The Alexandrian Greeks' tolerance for Ptolemy XII's courting of Roman support suddenly ended in 58 B.C.E. in the face of his passive reaction to Rome's annexation of Cyprus, the last piece of the Ptolemies' once great empire. Already embittered by the taxes he had levied to repay his Roman creditors, they rebelled and drove Ptolemy XII into exile.

While Ptolemy XII fled to Rome to seek the aid of his patron Pompey, his subjects proclaimed his wife, Cleopatra V Tryphaina, and his eldest daughter, Berenike, joint rulers and sent a large embassy headed by a philosopher named Dion to Rome to justify their actions. Not even Pompey could protect the king, however, when he arranged the assassination of Dion and most of the ambassadors. The enraged Senate ordered Ptolemy out of Italy and debated how to return him to Egypt. His exile finally ended in 55 B.C.E., when Aulus Gabinius, the governor of Syria, returned him to power by force.

Severe repression followed as Ptolemy XII sought to eliminate further resistance to his rule. Backed by a force of mercenaries left in Egypt by Gabinius—the so-called Gabinians—he took revenge on his enemies. As his wife was already dead, he ordered the execution of his daughter Berenike and her chief supporters, and confiscated their property. As that was not enough to repay the new loans he had contracted to persuade Gabinius to intervene in Egypt, Ptolemy XII even placed his principal creditor, a Roman moneylender named Gaius Rabirius Postumus, in charge of Egypt's finances and allowed him to extort vast sums of money and treasure from the country. Rabirius' reign of terror lasted for only a year, ending in 54 B.C.E. with his arrest and expulsion from Egypt. Ptolemy XII, however, held onto power for another four years.

Ptolemy XII's long and turbulent reign ended as it had begun, amid worry over the succession. The joint deification of his surviving children as the New Sibling Loving Gods (Theoi Neoi Philadelphoi) in 52 B.C.E. and his appointment of Cleopatra as his coregent the following year made clear his hope that his children would succeed him but did nothing to dispel the danger from Rome, heightened now by the huge debts he had contracted to secure his claim to the throne. Like Ptolemy X, Ptolemy XII made a will in favor of the Roman people, naming them not, however, as his heirs but as the collective guardian of his eldest son Ptolemy XIII and Cleopatra, who were to marry and to succeed him jointly as rulers of Egypt. After depositing one copy of his will in Alexandria for safekeeping and sending another to Pompey, who was to present it to the Senate for ratification, Ptolemy XII died in the spring of 51 B.C.E., having done all he could to provide for the survival of his dynasty.

CLEOPATRA ENTERS HISTORY (50–48 B.C.E.)

Cleopatra's marriage to her younger brother made her a public figure for the first time. Her father's decision that she should marry Ptolemy XIII is unlikely to have surprised or disturbed her or her brother. The shock and horror Greeks and Macedonians had felt in the 270s B.C.E. when Ptolemy II married his full sister Arsinoe II in accordance with Egyptian royal tradition had long since disappeared. For almost two centuries Cleopatra's ancestors had contracted such incestuous marriages in order to encourage their subjects to view them as special and to accept their divine status. By her time people would have been surprised if Ptolemy XII had not arranged such a marriage for his children. Nevertheless, there were serious obstacles to its success.

Although Ptolemy XII had intended that Cleopatra would serve as her ten-year-old brother's coregent, just as she had done during the final year of his own reign, this outcome was unlikely. Not only was she almost a decade older than Ptolemy XIII, but her life during the 50s B.C.E. had prepared her for power. While he was still a child, whose experience was limited to the artificial world of the palace at Alexandria, Cleopatra had spent her teenage years sharing her father's political struggles. She had experienced the humiliation Ptolemy XII had suffered at the hands of the Romans. She had also witnessed both his triumphant return to power in

54 B.C.E. and the fearful revenge he had taken on her sister and her supporters. Not surprisingly, Cleopatra quickly revealed that she would not
acquiesce in the supremacy of her brother and the court faction headed
by the eunuch Pothinos that made up his regency council.

Cleopatra asserted her claim to sole power soon after her father's death.
Her adoption of the title Thea Philopatora (Goddess Who Loves Her Father) proclaimed her to be his true successor. She also worked to build
support for her rule in Upper Egypt, where Ptolemy XII had enjoyed
strong backing. For almost two centuries Upper Egypt—especially the
Thebaid—had been a hotbed of Egyptian unrest. As recently as the early
80s B.C.E., Ptolemy X had brutally suppressed a native rebellion, destroying much of Thebes in the process. Like innumerable pharaohs before him, Ptolemy XII had sought support in the region by sponsoring
extensive temple-building activity in the great sanctuaries and cultivat-
ing the priestly and noble families, who treated temple and governmental offices as family possessions. The death of the old Buchis bull in 52
B.C.E. and the discovery of a new bull by Egyptian priests in early 51 B.C.E.
provided Cleopatra with the chance to continue her father's policies in
Upper Egypt, and she seized it.

Greeks and Romans found much to wonder at in Egyptian religion but
nothing puzzled and shocked them more than the cult of sacred animals.
Almost every deity was believed to be potentially embodied in particular animals. By the end of the first millennium B.C.E., devotion to sacred
animals had become central to popular cult, and reverence for them
could take extreme forms. The historian Diodoros, who visited Egypt in
60 B.C.E., saw a member of a Roman embassy torn to pieces by an enraged mob because he had accidentally killed a cat. A special place in
Egyptian religion, however, was occupied by a few animals, who were believed to be the living incarnations of particular gods. Such creatures
were identified by special markings and were unique. The death of one
and the discovery of its successor after a long search were occasions of
great rejoicing. During their lifetime, they were treated like pharaohs;
and after their death, they were mummified and splendidly buried in great
underground catacombs.

The Buchis bull was one of the most celebrated of these animals. Identified by his black face, white body with backward-growing hair, and his
supposed ability to change color hourly like a chameleon, Buchis was believed to be the incarnation of the solar god Montu of Hermonthis, a

city near Thebes. Cleopatra seized the opportunity offered by the installation of a new Buchis in 51 B.C.E. to secure for herself the loyalty of her father's Upper Egyptian supporters. Even decades later, during the reign of her conqueror—the Roman emperor Augustus—people remembered how "the Queen, the Lady of the Two Lands, the goddess who loves her father [Cleopatra], rowed him [Buchis] in the barque of Amun, together with the boats of the king, all the inhabitants of Thebes and Hermonthis and priests being with him."[2]

Cleopatra also secured the support of the Upper Egyptian aristocracy, powerful men such as Kallimakhos—the *strategos*, or governor, of Thebes and its environs. Cleopatra's venture into Upper Egypt was an unqualified success, as the Thebaid remained loyal to her throughout her long reign, even offering to rise in her support on the eve of Octavian's conquest of Egypt in 30 B.C.E. The center of political power in Ptolemaic Egypt was not, however, in the Thebaid but in the capital, Alexandria, whose turbulent citizen body had made and unmade kings for over a century. Unfortunately, Cleopatra had few followers in the capital.

Although Ptolemy XII had been the Alexandrian Greeks' choice for king in 80 B.C.E., relations between them had become increasingly bitter over the course of his reign, and Cleopatra inherited their hostility. Even more serious, her ambitions violated the traditions of her dynasty. Ptolemaic queens such as Arsinoe II and Cleopatra I had wielded great influence, but only as the consort or regent of a king. That meant that it was Ptolemy XIII and not Cleopatra who attracted the support of Ptolemaic loyalists; the most important of which were the Gabinians, who had kept her father in power during the final years of his reign. After his death, however, Cleopatra alienated them by her decision to surrender several Gabinians to the governor of Syria to face charges of murdering two sons of a prominent Roman politician.

The sources permit only a general outline of Cleopatra's struggle for power. At first, Cleopatra's speed and audacity worked to her advantage. For the last nine months of 51 B.C.E. and the first half of 50 B.C.E., her ascendancy is indicated by the disappearance of the name of Ptolemy XIII from official documents. By the fall of 50 B.C.E., however, Cleopatra's bold bid for sole power had clearly failed. Severe famine throughout Egypt caused by a disastrously low Nile had given her enemies their chance, and they had seized the opportunity to undermine her strong position in

Upper Egypt and strengthen their hold on popular opinion in Alexandria. A decree issued in October 50 B.C.E. in the name of Ptolemy XIII and Cleopatra ordered merchants to divert all grain collected in Upper Egypt to Alexandria, and threatened violators of the edict with death.

In desperation, Cleopatra may even have tried to find a more compliant royal husband by replacing Ptolemy XIII with her even younger brother, the future Ptolemy XIV. Some time in 49 B.C.E., however, she was forced to flee from Alexandria, taking refuge first in the Thebaid and then making her way to Palestine or southern Syria, where her father had had friends. After collecting a small army, she attempted to invade Egypt. Her advance was stopped at the border by the forces of her brother, however, which held the key fortress of Pelusium, enabling them to block the coastal road from Sinai into Egypt. Ironically, with final defeat imminent, Cleopatra was saved by the unexpected reappearance of Rome as a decisive factor in Egyptian affairs.

HITCHED TO CAESAR'S STAR: 48–44 B.C.E.

The struggle for power between Cleopatra and Ptolemy XIII coincided with the civil war between Julius Caesar and the Republican forces led by Ptolemy XII's patron, Pompey. Relations between Caesar and Pompey had deteriorated during the late 50s B.C.E. as Caesar's growing power and influence drove Pompey into alliance with the Senate. War had raged from early 49 B.C.E. until early summer 48 B.C.E., when Caesar decisively defeated Pompey and the senatorial forces at Pharsalus in northern Greece. Egypt had avoided direct involvement in the fighting, but the unexpected arrival in late July of ships bearing Pompey and his family at Pelusium with Caesar in hot pursuit threatened to drag Egypt into the conflict.

Pompey had good reason to expect a favorable reception from Ptolemy XIII and his regents. He had been the patron of Ptolemy XII and was the guardian of his will, which legitimized the reign of his son. A year earlier, when the outcome of the civil war was still in doubt, Ptolemy XIII's regents had provided Pompey's son Gnaeus Pompey with sixty war ships for his father's fleet. The ships had stayed in port at Corcyra in western Greece with the rest of the Republican fleet, fortunately leaving Egyptian neutrality intact. Pompey's defeat, however, changed the situation fundamentally. His patronage was no longer of any value, while giving him sanctuary in Egypt would alienate Caesar. Expediency trumped principle. Hoping to win Caesar's favor, Pothinos and the other regents decided to murder Pompey. Deceived by a former officer and friend in Egyptian service, Pompey was stabbed to death as he was being rowed to shore from his flagship. Pompey's decapitated body was left exposed on the beach, while the regents embalmed his head for presentation to Caesar as a gift.

The regents had badly miscalculated Caesar's reaction to Pompey's murder. Although Caesar had reason to be glad that his formidable rival had been removed from the scene without him being responsible, he affected grief and outrage when he arrived at Pelusium a few days later, turning away in disgust when he was presented with Pompey's head. He also wanted the money promised to him by Ptolemy XII in 59 B.C.E., which he needed for his campaigns against the remaining Republican forces.

Caesar made no effort to conceal the reality of Roman power over Egypt. He entered Alexandria like a consul visiting a subject city, declaring that he was now the executor of Ptolemy XII's will. Ptolemy XIII and Cleopatra were ordered to disband their armies and to submit their dispute over the throne to his judgment in Alexandria. The daring ruse by which Cleopatra had one of her followers smuggle her into the royal palace concealed in a load of bedclothes has led to endless speculation concerning Caesar's response to the sudden appearance of the charming young queen in his bedroom and the nature of their sex during the night that followed. Whatever actually happened, Ptolemy XIII understandably felt betrayed when he saw Cleopatra seated beside Caesar the next morning. With one audacious act, she had overcome her political eclipse and again gained a chance to secure her father's throne.

Caesar's resolution of their dispute revealed the full extent of Cleopatra's success. In accordance with the will of Ptolemy XII, he forced her brother to again accept her as his queen and co-ruler of Egypt. In an attempt to defuse hostility among the Alexandrians to his decision, Caesar also overturned Rome's annexation of Cyprus, returning the island to Ptolemaic authority and appointing as its rulers Cleopatra's other siblings, the future Ptolemy XIV and her remaining sister, Arsinoe.

There was a large element of bluff in Caesar's bold entry into Alexandria and assumption of power. In his haste to overtake Pompey, he had taken with him only ten Rhodian warships and four thousand troops, leaving the rest of his army behind in Greece. His audacity had temporarily defused opposition, but he underestimated both the sensitivity of the Alexandrian Greeks to any show of Roman power because of the humiliations they had experienced during the 50s B.C.E. and the astuteness of Ptolemy XIII's regency council. Once his enemies recognized Caesar's weakness, they besieged him in the royal palace.

Although the Alexandrian War receives little attention in Roman history, Caesar never came so close to death as during the battle for Alexandria. Caesar faced the classic nightmare of urban warfare. The guerilla tactics of the Alexandrian Greeks continually harassed him, while Ptolemy XIII's army advanced on the city. Battles raged around the harbor. Much of the area was destroyed by fire, including facilities connected to the famous Alexandrian library. Caesar once escaped certain death only by swimming from a sinking warship to safety. The nightmare ended in January 47 B.C.E., when a relieving army arrived in Egypt and lifted the siege.

Caesar's victory was also Cleopatra's victory. She had hitched her fate to Caesar's star when she made her theatrical appearance in his bedroom. She had remained loyally by his side in the palace throughout the siege, and she survived to enjoy the rewards of her loyalty. Cleopatra had already had the satisfaction of seeing the death of her principal enemies—Ptolemy XIII, who had been killed in battle, and Pothinos and the other leaders of his regency council, who had been executed on Caesar's orders. Her sister, Arsinoe, who had succeeded Ptolemy XIII as leader of the resistance to Caesar, was a prisoner, facing the humiliation of marching in Caesar's triumph whenever he finally returned to Rome. Cleopatra received her reward when Caesar appointed her and her ten-year-old brother, Ptolemy XIV, joint rulers of Egypt.

After almost four years of bitter struggle, Cleopatra had won. Although she was officially only the consort and queen of another of her brothers, Ptolemy XIV was only a figurehead without a regency council to protect his interests. Equally important, their marriage also reunited Egypt and Cyprus for the first time since 80 B.C.E., when it had been separated from Egypt, becoming an independent kingdom ruled by her father's unfortunate brother. Its reunification with Egypt marked the first step toward the achievement of what would be the major goal of Cleopatra's reign: the re-creation of the empire once ruled by her ancestors.

Cleopatra and Caesar celebrated their separate victories with a luxurious cruise up the Nile during which her subjects observed both their queen and the Roman protector who made her power possible. The Nile cruise was a brief but pleasant interlude. By the end of January 47 B.C.E., Caesar had left Egypt for Asia Minor to deal with an uprising in Pontus, leaving Cleopatra behind, pregnant with his son Caesarion.

Caesar also left in Egypt a strong occupation force of four legions, twenty thousand troops. Its stated purpose was to protect Cleopatra and her brother, who still lacked popular support in Alexandria. However, the staff officer who wrote a contemporary history of the Alexandrian War reveals that Caesar's real intentions for these troops were more complex, noting, "he considered . . . that the monarchs should be safeguarded by a garrison of our troops, if they remained loyal, while if they proved ungrateful, they could be coerced by this same garrison.[3] Caesar had made Cleopatra queen of Egypt, but she was on probation. She still had to prove herself to him.

Cleopatra and Caesar would not see each other again for over a year. Much happened in the interval, but the sources provide few details. Two events, however, stand out. The first was Cleopatra's decision to begin construction of the Caesareum near the harbor at Alexandria, a huge temple in mixed Egyptian and Greek style devoted to the worship of Caesar. It would be a perpetual reminder to the Alexandrians and to all who visited Alexandria of the personal link between her and Caesar and his support for her regime. The other was the birth on June 23, 47 B.C.E., of her son Caesarion, who embodied her hopes for the continuation of her dynasty. Following the lead of her father, who had himself deified as the living incarnation of Dionysos, Cleopatra celebrated the birth of Caesarion by identifying him with the god Horus, whom Egyptians believed was incarnate in every king, and herself with the goddess Isis—Horus's mother and the wife of Osiris, the king of the dead. Coins struck on Cyprus in 47 B.C.E. show Cleopatra with the attributes of Isis and Aphrodite nursing the infant Caesarion.

Early in 46 B.C.E., Cleopatra visited Rome with her husband, Ptolemy XIV, at the invitation of Caesar, who housed them across the Tiber in his suburban estate in present day Trastevere.[4] Her visit was brief and the results mixed. The highlight was certainly Caesar persuading the Senate to reward her loyalty by granting her and her brother the status of allied kings and friends of the Roman people. Less satisfactory for her was Caesar's spectacular triumph for his victories over Gaul, Egypt, Pontus, and

Mauretania in July 46 B.C.E. The Roman populace's unexpected sympathy at the pathetic spectacle of her sister, Arsinoe, loaded with chains in the triumphal procession induced Caesar to spare her life, sentencing her instead to exile in the famous Temple of Artemis at Ephesus. As long as Arsinoe was alive, she was a threat to Cleopatra's plans. Still, when Cleopatra returned to Egypt later that summer, she could be satisfied with the results of her first visit to Rome. Caesar had not denied that Caesarion was their child, and he had confirmed the independence of Egypt that her father had struggled so hard to achieve.

Cleopatra was back in Rome together with Caesarion a little over a year later. The reason for her second trip to Rome is unknown. She may have hoped to gain formal recognition from Caesar of his paternity of Caesarion. Attitudes toward her in Rome had hardened significantly since her last visit, however. Political unrest over Caesar's autocratic rule was rapidly increasing, and the presence of Cleopatra and her son added fuel to the fire. Beneficial reforms—such as Caesar's replacement of the hopelessly inefficient Roman lunar calendar with the Egyptian solar calendar we still use today—and unprecedented honors—such as placing a statue of Cleopatra in the temple of his divine ancestress Venus Genetrix (Venus the mother)—caused equal offense. Rumors abounded that Caesar was seeking legislation to allow him to marry the Egyptian queen as part of a plan to move the capital of the empire from Rome to Alexandria. His sudden assassination on March 15, 44 B.C.E., and the turmoil at Rome that followed made her understandably insecure. By mid-April, Cleopatra and Caesarion had left Rome for Egypt.

BETWEEN A ROCK AND A HARD PLACE: 44–41 B.C.E.

Caesar's assassination opened a period of upheaval in Rome. Within a year, hostilities had broken out throughout the empire between Caesar's heirs and their supporters and the Republican forces led by his assassins, Brutus and Cassius. Cleopatra faced particularly difficult choices in the new situation. Her personal history would have led her to side with the Caesarian faction in the coming civil war. However, the suspicions of his grandnephew and heir Octavian, who viewed Caesarion as a potential rival, made her cautious. Meanwhile Cassius' occupation of Syria and alliance with the Iranian empire of Parthia threatened Egypt's security from outside, while famine—the Nile flood was disastrously low in both 43 and 42 B.C.E.—and plague undermined the internal stability of the kingdom. Last but not least, Ptolemy XIV was growing up and might assert his claim to rule at any time.

Cleopatra responded vigorously and effectively to these challenges. She first neutralized potential opposition in Egypt. Shortly after her return to Alexandria in summer 44 B.C.E., Cleopatra had Caesarion proclaimed king as Ptolemy Caesarion Theos Philopator and Philometor (the god, who loves his father and his mother). About the same time, Ptolemy XIV died mysteriously. Rumor accused Cleopatra—probably correctly—of poisoning him. Whatever the truth of the charge, the reality was that with her husband dead and her infant son as her co-regent, Cleopatra's hold on power was finally secure. Her efforts earlier in the decade to build political support in Egypt also bore fruit. Aggressive efforts to provide food to the suffering Egyptian population by her supporters in Upper Egypt such as Kallimakhos, the powerful governor of Thebes, combined with Cleopatra's own relief efforts in Alexandria prevented serious unrest during the famine years of the late 40s B.C.E. Security in Egypt also strengthened Cleopatra's hand in dealing with the mounting external threats to her kingdom.

Although Cleopatra's sympathies lay with the Caesarians, the welfare of Egypt depended on her avoiding being drawn into the hostilities that broke out in 43 B.C.E. She tried, therefore, to assist the forces of the Second Triumvirate without attracting the wrath of the Republicans. It was a delicate diplomatic dance, and the results were uneven. Cleopatra turned over the four legions Caesar had left in Egypt in 48 B.C.E. to the triumviral general Dolabella's representative. As a reward for her loyalty, the triumvirs recognized Caesarion as Cleopatra's co-ruler.

Cassius, however, seized control of the four legions before they could join the main triumviral forces in Europe, leaving Cleopatra facing a serious military threat on Egypt's northeast frontier. Her plea that famine and plague prevented her from actively supporting Cassius only encouraged his dream of invading Egypt. Her vulnerability was increased still further by the defection to Cassius of Serapion, her governor of Cyprus. Only Brutus' summons of Cassius to the Balkans in 42 B.C.E. to prepare for the upcoming battle with the triumvirs saved Egypt from invasion and certain defeat. Freed from the threat of invasion, Cleopatra finally joined openly the Caesarian cause, personally leading a large fleet to Greece.

Unfortunately, a storm destroyed most of her ships at sea, forcing Cleopatra to return to Egypt without aiding the triumvirs in the campaign that ended at the Battle of Philippi, with the decisive defeat of the Republican cause and the death of Brutus and Cassius.

CLEOPATRA AND ANTONY: ALLIES AND LOVERS (41–37 B.C.E.)

Cleopatra, therefore, had reason for concern, when Mark Antony ordered her to come to Tarsus in southern Turkey in 41 B.C.E. to answer charges that she had aided Cassius. By itself, her plea that Cassius had threatened Egypt and that a storm had frustrated her attempt to support the triumvirs was weak. Cleopatra did, however, know Antony and, more important, his weaknesses and how to take advantage of them.

Roman legend claimed that the fifteen-year old Cleopatra first met and charmed Antony when he was a dashing cavalry officer in Gabinius' army, which returned Ptolemy XII to power, but this is unlikely. She would certainly have met him during her visits to Rome—especially in 44 B.C.E., when Antony served as Caesar's consul and chief aide—and become familiar with his personality, in which great courage and sensuality mingled with his strong belief in his personal descent from Herakles. Antony's belief in his closeness to the divine was further enhanced when the priests of Artemis of Ephesus proclaimed him the living incarnation of Dionysos shortly before his epochal meeting with Cleopatra in 41 B.C.E.

Cleopatra made good use of her knowledge of Antony's personality. Instead of playing the part of a humble suppliant like other eastern rulers and dynasts, she boldly assumed the role of the Egyptian royal goddess Isis in the guise of the Greek goddess Aphrodite coming to visit her husband Osiris in his manifestation as Dionysos. The Greek biographer Plutarch's brilliant description of this spectacular extravaganza has focused attention on the night of banqueting and sex that followed their meeting instead of the hard political bargaining that took place during and after it.

Mark Antony was at the peak of his prestige and power when he and Cleopatra met at Tarsus. As the senior member of the Second Triumvirate and the chief architect of its victory at the Battle of Philippi, he far overshadowed Octavian and Marcus Lepidus. Antony used his preeminence to take for himself the choicest parts of the Roman Empire: Gaul and, especially, the eastern Mediterranean, with its rich provinces and client kingdoms. During his trip to Tarsus, he rewrote the political map of the region, rewarding those astute enough to join the winning side in time and levying heavy financial penalties on the less perceptive. Dominance of Rome's eastern territories, however, also brought with it the challenge of dealing with Parthia.

Masters of an empire that stretched from Mesopotamia to the borders of India, the Parthians had crushed an invading Roman army in 54 B.C.E. led by Marcus Crassus, at the Battle of Carrhae. During the recent war, the Parthians had been allies of Cassius and a small Parthian contingent had even fought on the Republican side at Philippi. Caesar had been preparing a grand expedition against Parthia at the time of his death in 44 B.C.E. For Antony, the temptation to assume Caesar's mantle, avenge Crassus, secure Rome's eastern frontier, and win glory equal to that of Alexander the Great was too tempting to pass up.

The support of Egypt—the largest and wealthiest of Rome's client states—and her queen was essential to the success of Antony's plans. Antony, therefore, accepted Cleopatra's claim that Serapion, her governor of Cyprus, had acted on his own in aiding Cassius. Cleopatra, for her part, willingly accepted the opportunity offered her by Antony, surrendering Serapion for execution and demanding only the execution of her sister, Arsinoe—who had lived under the protection of the goddess Artemis at Ephesus since 46 B.C.E.—and the death of a young man who had been wandering through Syria and Palestine claiming to be Ptolemy XIII, miraculously saved from the Battle of the Nile.

Cleopatra's personal diplomacy had been a brilliant success. She had dodged the bullet that threatened her, eliminated her last potential rival, and found a powerful new patron and protector in Antony. Cleopatra celebrated her escape by inviting Antony to spend the winter of 40 B.C.E. with her in Egypt. As usual, the sources treat Antony's decision to go to Egypt instead of confronting Parthian raiders in Syria as evidence of his growing enslavement by Cleopatra. In support, they cite Antony and Cleopatra's formation of a social club called the Society of Inimitable Livers and their extravagant and riotous parties. Cleopatra's cook is reported to have claimed that every meal had to be perfect for the members of the society, and that he had to prepare huge amounts of food for even the smallest party in case some dish became spoiled.

The reality of Antony's long stay in Egypt was different. He delegated dealing with the Parthian raids to his subordinates, who defeated and drove them back across the Euphrates. Meanwhile, Antony courted the support of the Alexandrian Greeks, carefully avoiding Caesar's mistakes by eschewing all signs of Roman authority and wearing Greek dress in public. At the same time, Cleopatra spared no effort in encouraging his plans for an invasion of Parthia. Before they could put their plans into effect, however, events in Italy forced Antony to return to the west in 40 B.C.E., leaving Cleopatra pregnant with twins, whom she named Alexander the Sun (Helios) and Cleopatra the Moon (Selene). The twin's names revealed Cleopatra's hope that her alliance would help Antony repeat the glorious achievements of Alexander the Great by conquering the new Iranian empire of Parthia.

Three years would pass before they saw each other again. Much changed in that interval. Open warfare between the forces of Octavian and those of Antony had only been averted by difficult negotiations in which Antony agreed to marry Octavian's sister Octavia. He also conceded to Octavian control of Italy and the provinces of Spain and Gaul. Antony's marriage kept the peace for the time being, but he desperately needed a major military success to counter Octavian's growing power in the west.

While Antony's superiority over Octavian was declining, Cleopatra's position in Egypt was gradually improving. The details are lost, but the extensive program of temple and monument building Cleopatra undertook in Upper Egypt and Alexandria in honor of herself and Caesarion indicates that she took advantage of her kingdom's recovery from the famine and plague years of the late 40s B.C.E. to build support for her regime in the traditional pharaonic manner. With her hold on Egypt secure, Cleopatra's position was much stronger when Antony summoned her to Antioch to discuss his planned invasion of Parthia than it had been at the time of their first meeting at Tarsus four years earlier.

The ancient sources rightly point to the renewal of Cleopatra's affair with Antony as one of the main results of her stay at Antioch during the fall of 37 B.C.E. and the winter of 36 B.C.E. Cleopatra won Antony's recognition of Alexander Helios and Cleopatra Selene as his children; and when she returned to Egypt the next spring, she was pregnant again with his child. Cleopatra also achieved major political successes at Antioch. In preparation for the Parthian expedition, Antony carried out the most

extensive reorganization of the Roman east since the 60s B.C.E., rewarding loyal client kings and removing those suspected of Parthian sympathies. As ruler of the largest and most important client kingdom,
Cleopatra emerged as the big winner in the process. In addition to confirming her authority over Cyprus, Antony put under Egyptian rule an
enormous swath of territory, including the island of Crete, Kyrene in
modern Libya, numerous cities in Phoenicia, Syria and Cilicia in southern Turkey, and the Arab kingdom of Iturea in northern Palestine.

Not for over a century had Egyptian power extended so far. Cleopatra
presided over an empire almost as large as that of her great third-century
B.C.E. ancestors. She treated the concessions of Antioch as the beginning
of a new era. On her return to Egypt, she announced that a new era of
greatness had begun in 37 B.C.E., and assumed two new titles to celebrate
Egypt's renewed empire. The first, Thea Neotera (the younger goddess),
recalled her ancestress Cleopatra Thea, the daughter of Ptolemy VI, who
had reigned over many of these territories a century earlier as the wife of
three Seleukid monarchs. Her other title, Philopatris (the lover of her
country), affirmed her devotion to Egypt and its welfare. Finally, by naming the son she bore later in 36 B.C.E. Ptolemy Philadelphos, Cleopatra
honored the greatest of her ancestors and the founder of her dynasty's
imperial greatness.

Not surprisingly, Antony's detractors in Rome viewed the concessions
of Antioch as further evidence of his enslavement by Cleopatra. The
truth was otherwise. Coins minted in various cities and given to Egypt
bore images of both Cleopatra and Antony with Roman military titles,
emphasizing that he had acted in his capacity as a Roman official in expanding Egyptian authority in the Near East. In addition, Cleopatra did
not gain all that she wished from Antony. Control over Judaea—lost to
Ptolemaic authority since 197 B.C.E.—was essential to connect her new
possessions to Egypt; but Antony had recognized Herod the Great as king
of Judaea in 41 B.C.E., and he steadfastly refused to strip Herod of his
kingdom despite all of Cleopatra's pleas and intrigues against the Jewish
monarch in the years after 37 B.C.E. She had to be content with a piece
of the kingdom of the Nabataean Arabs south of Judaea and some valuable balsam groves near the ancient city of Jericho, which she leased back
to Herod for a high fee.

The concessions of Antioch marked the high point of Cleopatra's
reign. As her failure to move Antony on Judaea revealed, however,

Cleopatra's hold on her new territories was precarious. Although Cleopatra had re-created the empire of her great third-century ancestors, she ruled it at the pleasure of Rome as represented by Antony. Should she lose his favor, all would be lost. Preventing that from happening obsessed Cleopatra during the final years of her reign.

THE FINAL YEARS: 36–30 B.C.E.

If Cleopatra were to maintain control of her new empire, it was essential that Antony retain his primacy in the Second Triumvirate, which required that he win a great victory against the Parthians. Unfortunately for Cleopatra, the long-planned-for Parthian campaign ended in total failure.

At first, everything seemed to be going well. Preparations for the campaign were on a grand scale. Antony collected an army of almost a hundred thousand troops—including sixteen legions of infantry and ten thousand cavalry—and arranged alliances with the kings of Armenia and Media. The grand army left Syria in May 36 B.C.E., and penetrated deeply into Parthian territory, only to fritter away its early success in an unsuccessful siege of Phraaspa, the Parthian capital, that lasted into October, when Antony decided to return to Roman territory. Harsh winter weather, Parthian harassment, and the treachery of Antony's Armenian and Median allies transformed the retreat into a nightmare.

Antony displayed all of his courage and his superb leadership qualities during the long retreat. By the time the army reached the security of Syria, Antony had lost more than thirty thousand men—over a third of his force. The magnitude of the military and political disaster he had suffered was obvious to all, especially since at almost the same time, Octavian ended the last vestiges of the civil war by decisively defeating the forces of Sextus Pompey at Cape Naulochus in Sicily. Although Antony still had almost twenty-five legions under his command, he had lost the initiative to Octavian and would never regain it. As a result, the failure of the great Parthian expedition opened a period of unprecedented danger for Cleopatra and her family that would only end with her death five years later in 30 B.C.E.

The decline in Antony's political fortunes made itself felt immediately. Octavian consolidated his power in the west by stripping Lepidus of his remaining territories without consulting Antony. He also broke his promise to provide twenty-thousand troops for the Parthian campaign, sending Antony instead some ships captured from Sextus Pompey and a mere two thousand soldiers, who were to be brought to Antony by his wife Octavia. Faced with public humiliation by Octavian, Antony responded with defiance. On reaching Athens, Octavia received a message ordering her to return to Rome but to send the soldiers to Egypt.

The ancient sources, hostile as always to Cleopatra, describe in vivid detail the wiles she used to force a breach between Antony and his wife. The stories may even be true, but little persuasion was needed. Antony's marriage to Octavia had been a marriage of political convenience, and the rapidly deteriorating relations between Antony and Octavian stripped it of any value. Indeed, if Antony had allowed Octavia to proceed to Alexandria with the paltry force of soldiers Octavian had sent with her, he would have publicly admitted his inferiority to his brother-in-law. The redistribution of power within the Second Triumvirate had forced Antony and Cleopatra together; it was their only hope of survival.

Even as Octavian was consolidating his power in Italy and the west, Cleopatra and Antony were to enjoy one last moment of glory. The king of the Medes fell out with the Parthians over the division of the spoils from Antony's failed campaign and signaled a willingness to switch sides and support Rome in a future invasion of Parthia. When the king of Armenia refused Antony's offer of an alliance that would be sealed by a marriage between Alexander Helios and his daughter, Antony invaded Armenia in the spring of 34 B.C.E.

Cleopatra accompanied the army to the Euphrates and then returned to Egypt, stopping at Jerusalem on the way. Herod would claim later in his memoirs that Cleopatra tried to seduce him while he gallantly refused to follow the advice of his council and murder her when he had the chance. Whatever the truth of Herod's self-serving claims, nothing untoward happened, and Cleopatra left Judaea after a brief stay. Antony, meanwhile, achieved a complete victory in Armenia, capturing the king and most of his family, and bringing them back to Egypt as prisoners.

Antony's conquest of Armenia was the occasion for the last great royal spectacle staged in Alexandria. Wearing a crown of ivy and carrying a *thyrsos* as befitted the living incarnation of Dionysos, Antony entered Alexandria and presented his army and his royal prisoners, who were bound in golden chains, to Cleopatra. The ceremony reached its climax in the great gymnasium of Alexandria, where Cleopatra and her children, seated on gold thrones on a silver stage, received from Antony rule over the Roman east and the territories Antony planned to conquer.

Armenia and Parthia were assigned to Alexander Helios, who appeared dressed in the garb of the Persian kings of old. Ptolemy Philadelphos received all Roman territory from Egypt to the Hellespont, while Caesarion was recognized as the legitimate son of Julius Caesar with the title King of Kings. Cleopatra Selene received Kyrenaika and part of Crete. Finally, Cleopatra was proclaimed Queen of Kings and ruler of Egypt. Coins issued at Alexandria in honor of these events celebrated Antony as the conqueror of Armenia and Cleopatra as "Queen of Kings, whose sons are kings," and as "Queen and the Youngest Goddess." Although Antony still retained his position as triumvir, the donations of Alexandria leave no doubt that he dreamed of something far more grandiose, nothing less than to re-create for Rome the empire of Alexander the Great with Cleopatra and their children as his partners in its rule, but it was not to be.

Octavian exploited news of the donations of Alexandria to launch a fierce propaganda offensive against Antony. Octavian minimized the significance of Antony's conquest of Armenia, while condemning him for betraying Roman tradition by celebrating a triumph in Alexandria instead of Rome and illegally granting territory belonging to the Roman people to Cleopatra and her children. Antony responded in kind, accusing Octavian of treachery and debauchery. One casualty of the increasingly bitter feud was Antony's wife, Octavia. Antony took the initiative in severing the last link between him and Octavian, sending Octavia a notice of divorce and summarily ordering her to vacate his house in Rome. Marriage to Cleopatra quickly followed, thereby publicly sealing his alliance with the Egyptian queen and his defiance of Octavian.

Both sides began to prepare openly for war in 32 B.C.E. With bitter memories of the recent civil wars fresh in the minds of Romans, Octavian studiously ignored Antony, treating him merely as the slave of Cleopatra's lust for power. Octavian even seized Antony's will from the custody of the vestal virgins. Once in possession of the will, Octavian revealed to an outraged Senate that in it not only did Antony reaffirm the gifts of Roman territory he had given Cleopatra and assert that Caesarion was Caesar's son, but that his subservience to Cleopatra was so great that he had even provided that if he died in Rome his body was to be taken to Alexandria for burial. Rumors that Cleopatra's favorite oath was "when I give judgment on the Capitol" in Rome further heightened hostility toward her. War was declared, therefore, on Cleopatra, whom Octavian portrayed as an enemy of Rome on the scale of the great Carthaginian general Hannibal. Not everyone, of course, was deceived by Octavian's propaganda. Both consuls for the year 32 B.C.E. and over two hundred Senators—almost a quarter of the Senate—joined Antony and Cleopatra in Egypt. The final struggle for the legacy of Julius Caesar had begun, and on its outcome hinged the fate of Cleopatra and her dynasty.

Cleopatra played a prominent role when hostilities actually began in 31 B.C.E., commanding the Egyptian fleet in person and participating openly in Antony's war council. Antony's Roman supporters pleaded with him to send her back to Egypt, pointing out the credence her presence with the army gave to Octavian's propaganda. Antony rejected their advice, however. Cleopatra's ships formed the core of his fleet, and it was her wealth that paid his troops. Some of his Asian allies may even have seen in her the agent of their revenge for all the suffering brought on them by almost a century of Roman oppression.[5]

On paper, Cleopatra and Antony's chances for victory were good. Their enormous forces—five hundred warships and thirty legions plus auxiliaries—were superior to those of their enemies. Antony, however, repeated Pompey's mistake of 48 B.C.E. by choosing to fight a defensive campaign in Greece instead of carrying the war to Octavian in Italy. Octavian and his brilliant general Marcus Agrippa took full advantage of the opportunity afforded them by Antony's strategy, and by late summer 31 B.C.E., Antony's naval forces were blockaded in the bay of Actium in western Greece.

The Battle of Actium on September 2, 31 B.C.E. was the last major naval battle of antiquity. Over six hundred ships took part. The Roman poet Virgil treated it in the *Aeneid*—Rome's national epic—as a clash of civilizations in which Octavian and the Roman gods preserved Italy from conquest by Cleopatra and the barbaric animal-headed gods of Egypt. Octavian celebrated his victory by founding a city named Nicopolis (victory city) at Actium and displaying thirty-six metal rams from the ships captured or sunk in the battle on a great monument built on the site of his camp, whose ruins have recently been discovered. The truth was less glorious. Although her enemies claimed that Cleopatra cravenly abandoned Antony at the height of the battle, the fact that their ships put to sea with their sails on board instead of left onshore as was usual in battle indicates that they had decided to try to save their fleet by breaking Octavian's blockade. As it turned out, only the Egyptian fleet and some of Antony's other ships succeeded in escaping. The rest surrendered, as did most of Antony's army in Greece soon afterward.

It was almost a year before Octavian's army entered Alexandria in August 30 B.C.E. During the interval, Antony fell into a deep depression, while Cleopatra struck out at suspected enemies, executing the king of Armenia and his family as well as prominent members of the Alexandrian aristocracy who roused her suspicions. A plan to escape to India ended in failure, when the Nabataeans, some of whose territory she had acquired from Antony in 37 B.C.E., took their revenge by sinking her ships as they emerged from the old canal that Ptolemy II had built to link the Nile to the Red Sea. She and Antony reconstituted their old society of Inimitable Livers as the club of Those Who Will Die Together as the Roman armies advanced on Egypt. In the end, she barricaded herself and her treasure in her tomb in Alexandria to await the end.

Behind the scenes, however, Cleopatra conducted feverish negotiations with Octavian, most likely about her ultimate fate and, especially, that of her family. Even if she couldn't secure her own life, Cleopatra may have hoped to persuade Octavian to allow Caesarion to rule Egypt as a client king. Certainly, it was to that end that she rebuffed offers by her Upper Egyptian supporters to fight against the Romans. Ancient and some modern historians have even suggested that she was the source of the rumor of her death that drove Antony to suicide, although that is unlikely. Octavian allowed her to bury Antony, but a personal meeting with him seems to have disabused Cleopatra of any hope of a reprieve. If she lived, Octavian intended to take her to Rome to march in his triumph as her sister Arsinoe had done in that of Julius Caesar sixteen years earlier. With all hope gone, Cleopatra committed suicide on August 12, 30 B.C.E.

The manner of Cleopatra's death has mystified historians since antiquity. The familiar story that she died of the bite of a snake first appeared in a tableau showing her being bitten by a cobra that Octavian displayed in his triumph in 27 B.C.E. No trace of a snake was found at the time of her death, however, and it is difficult to imagine how a cobra could have been smuggled in to her, or how one snake could have been responsible for her death and that of the two female servants who died with her. It is more likely that they all took some kind of poison. She was thirty-nine years old. However it happened, her suicide may have saved the lives of at least some of her children.

Nothing could have saved Caesarion, since his claim to be a son of Julius Caesar made him a potential threat to Octavian. Betrayed by his tutor while trying to escape to Nubia, he was brought back to Alexandria and executed. Cleopatra's other children, however, survived, and were raised by Antony's former wife, Octavia. Cleopatra Selene even grew up to become a queen herself, marrying Juba II, the king of Mauretania in North Africa. Their son Ptolemy succeeded his father and ruled his kingdom until he was executed in 40 C.E. by the Roman emperor Caligula. His death finally ended the long line of Ptolemies, whose glory Cleopatra had struggled so hard to reestablish.

CHAPTER 3

PTOLEMAIC EGYPT: HOW DID IT WORK?

The recent discovery of a papyrus with a sample of Cleopatra's hand-writing created a sensation. Although she had written only one word—*ginestho*, "let it be so"—at the end of the document, the document is of great interest because it provides historians with a rare glimpse of Cleopatra at work. After all, her glamorous affairs with Julius Caesar and Mark Antony occupied only a relatively small part of her long reign in comparison to the time she spent as queen of Egypt.

The papyrus contains a royal decree with a subscription in Cleopatra's own handwriting ordering that it be enforced. The decree was issued in February 33 B.C.E. and instructs government officials to ensure that privileges awarded by Cleopatra to a member of a Roman senatorial family named Quintus Cascellius be honored. According to the decree, Cascellius was granted the right to export substantial amounts of grain from Egypt and import wine tax-free. In addition, his lands were also to be tax-free, and his tenants—together with their work animals and the Nile boats he used to transport his grain and wine—were to be exempt from government service.

Cleopatra's purpose in issuing this decree was obviously to encourage the loyalty of a member of a distinguished Roman family. Unfortunately, we do not know if she was successful. The decree does, however, reveal her at work doing the unglamorous but essential business of governing Egypt: reviewing public documents, providing for their transmission to the appropriate offices, and ensuring that their provisions were enforced. Except for the fact that Cascellius was a Roman, nothing distinguishes this decree from the innumerable other such documents Cleopatra must have dictated, reviewed, and subscribed during her reign. As the document's editor noted, for Cleopatra to fulfill these duties, "she would have had to work round the clock."[1]

Many of these duties were religious. As pharaoh, she and her predecessors played an active role in the religious life of Egypt, fulfilling the Egyptian king's traditional duty of performing the rituals and ceremonies believed necessary to ensure the survival not only of Egypt but of the world itself. Similarly, in their capacity as successors of Alexander the Great as Macedonian kings, they also officiated at the numerous festivals and sacrifices in honor of the Greek gods that were celebrated at Alexandria. Other duties were ceremonial, such as greeting subjects, receiving petitions, welcoming ambassadors, and appointing officials to office. The bulk of a monarch's time, however, was occupied by duties that were invisible to his or her subjects but essential to the governance of Egypt, namely, those connected with the position of head of government. Until relatively recently, however, the details of the Ptolemaic government of Egypt were almost unknown.

PAPYRI AND PTOLEMAIC EGYPT

Discovering how the Ptolemies actually governed Egypt is one of the great achievements of modern historical research. It required the efforts of historians from many countries during the late nineteenth and twentieth centuries and even the creation of a whole new science known as papyrology. This effort was necessary because of a fundamental difference in the goals of ancient and modern historiography. While modern historians believe all subjects can be treated historically, ancient historians aimed to tell stories of action. The result was a narrow focus on political and military history.

Today, social history, economic history, or administrative history are the subjects of whole subdisciplines of history. In antiquity, however, they were not considered suitable topics for historical works. Except for the occasional anecdote that might throw light on the character of a king or queen, therefore, Greek and Roman historians ignored these subjects in their works. The discovery by archaeologists of documents—such as the decree for Cascellius—written on a variety of materials—stone inscriptions, ostraka (pieces of broken pottery), and especially papyrus—has filled this gap and revealed the nature of the government of Egypt under the Ptolemies.

Throughout most of antiquity, papyrus was the standard writing material in Egypt and the eastern Mediterranean basin. It was a paperlike material made from strips cut from the papyrus reed, and provided an excellent medium for writing, but one whose long-term survival required that it be protected from damp, mold, and other threats. Only the dry desert climate of Egypt has allowed papyrus documents to survive in substantial numbers. Ancient papyri first began to reach Europe in the eighteenth century c.e. It was only with the beginnings of systematic excavation of Egyptian sites in the nineteenth century c.e., however, that large numbers of papyri were discovered, and their significance as sources for Egyptian history was recognized.

While papyri have restored to us many lost literary works—such as poems of the Greek poetess Sappho—and have provided valuable information about the whole range of the lives of the inhabitants of Ptolemaic Egypt, they are particularly informative about the multifarious activities of the Ptolemaic government of Egypt. Administrative organization and policy, tax collection, religious affairs, and legal proceedings are all illuminated by papyri. Moreover, since the Egyptian populace encountered representatives of the Ptolemaic government on an almost daily basis, this rich documentation provides us with snapshots of the Ptolemaic government at work, from the royal court to the smallest Egyptian village.

Most but not all papyri are written in Greek and document the lives of the privileged Greek minority in Ptolemaic Egypt. Although detailed study of the numerous Demotic (vernacular Egyptian) papyri has barely begun, it has already made clear that despite the influx of Greeks, the Egyptian way of life, legal system, and religious institutions all endured and even flourished in Ptolemaic Egypt. Unfortunately, while papyri have done much to compensate for the deficiencies of the literary sources for the history of Cleopatra and her dynasty, their evidence is often incomplete and hard to interpret.

The problem is that there are significant gaps in the papyrological evidence. The first and most serious gap is the almost total lack of papyri from Alexandria, the capital of Ptolemaic Egypt, because the high water table in the area has destroyed them. The vast majority of papyri have been discovered instead in Middle and Upper Egypt, particularly in the waste dumps and cemeteries of the new towns and villages the Ptolemies founded for Greek immigrants in the depression west of the Nile known as the Fayum. The result is that we see the Ptolemaic government only as it is reflected in the provinces; it is as if historians were trying to analyze the government of the United States based only on evidence from rural Kansas. Chance has also played a large role in determining what periods and topics historians can study with the aid of papyri.

A good example is provided by a famous and informative batch of papyri found at the site of Tebtunis in the Fayum. During excavations there in 1900 for the University of California, Berkeley, and the Hearst Foundation, Egyptian workmen discovered a cemetery full of mummified crocodiles. One of the workmen, furious because there was no reward for mummified crocodiles, savagely hacked open one of the crocodiles, revealing that it was filled with papyri from the second and first centuries B.C.E. The papyri turned out to be discarded records from the office of a royal scribe named Menches and provided invaluable information about both the duties of royal scribes and the village of Kerkeosiris in which Menches lived and worked. If that workman had not become so frustrated at his "bad luck," historians would lack the most important extant body of evidence for studying the life of an Egyptian village in Ptolemaic Egypt in the late Ptolemaic period.[2]

THE ORGANIZATION OF PTOLEMAIC EGYPT

Ptolemy I hit the jackpot when he gained control of Egypt. The fifth century B.C.E. historian Herodotos claimed that Egypt had more wonders than any country in the world. Essentially a gigantic oasis watered by the Nile, Egypt was richer in history and resources and more densely populated than any other country known to the Greeks. Four centuries later, another Greek historian named Diodoros claimed that during Cleopatra's reign, almost seven million Egyptians lived in more than thirty thousand towns. Although the numbers are certainly exaggerated, they give a vivid idea of the impression Egypt made on visitors. Governing such a vast country required the Ptolemies to develop the extensive and complex administrative system revealed by the papyri.

The Ptolemies were autocrats, who ruled Egypt simultaneously as successors of the pharaohs and Macedonian kings. Their dual roles not only guaranteed their power over both Egyptians and Greeks, but also meant that they had a relatively free hand in developing their administrative system, since Egypt and its native and immigrant population literally belonged to them. Nevertheless, the Ptolemies did not create a new administration from scratch, but built on the foundations laid by their Egyptian predecessors.

One reality determined governmental organization throughout Egyptian history: the pharaohs and the gods were the greatest landowners in Egypt. All Egypt was their estate and provided the revenues needed to enable the kings to govern the country and perform the rituals and ceremonies essential to the survival not only of Egypt but of the world itself. Grants of royal land paid officials and provided the economic basis for the innumerable temples whose priests served as the king's deputies in the worship of the gods. Although the extent of temple holdings during the Ptolemaic period is unknown, only they rivaled the government in the size of their holdings. Their workshops produced a variety of goods needed for their ceremonies and for trade, including fine textiles, metals, and papyri. Not surprisingly, the priests of the greatest temples formed a tiny but wealthy and influential native elite.

The Egyptian populace on whose labor both the government and temples depended lived in the towns and villages of Egypt. These were grouped into territorial units called nomes—whose number varied from 36 to 40—each of which was administered by an official historian called a nomarch. The nomarch was responsible for maintaining order in his nome, collecting and forwarding taxes to the central government, and judging disputes that were referred to him. In carrying out his tasks, the nomarch was assisted by a varied body of officials including village scribes, elders and village headmen, tax collectors, and police officials.

Although local officials received new Greek titles to replace their offices' venerable Egyptian titles, the Ptolemies otherwise retained this organization essentially unchanged from the establishment of the dynasty in the late fourth century B.C.E. until the Roman conquest in 30 B.C.E. What they did do, however, was superimpose on it a new centralized administrative system for Egypt as a whole that was based on the principle that the king's work takes priority over all other activities. Although the first hints of the new system were already apparent during the reign of Ptolemy I, its chief architect was his successor, Ptolemy II.

Ptolemy II based his new system on the rigorous exploitation of Egypt's rich agricultural land—land so rich that Herodotos believed that Egyptians grew crops without work. The first historians to study the Ptolemaic government of Egypt believed that in order to achieve his goals, Ptolemy II thoroughly reorganized the Egyptian economy, transforming and modernizing the barter-based economy of pharaonic Egypt by the introduction of coinage on a large scale. Land usage also was rationalized by the introduction of a comprehensive classification system according to which all Egyptian land was divided into two broad categories: royal land for basic agricultural production and "released land." There were four subcategories of released land, which were defined by their function: (1) cleruchic land to support the army; (2) gift land to reward government officials; (3) temple land to support Egypt's numerous temples; and (4) private land, which included personal house and garden plots owned by individuals.

The nonagricultural sectors of the economy were also tightly organized. Major areas of the economy such as textile, papyrus, and oil production were organized as state monopolies, intended to generate the maximum revenue for the king from fees and taxes. Aggressive efforts were made to minimize foreign competition for the profits of Egyptian commerce. Strict currency controls were imposed that required that all foreign coinage be exchanged for Egyptian coinage at artificially low rates. Similarly, government regulations limited the amount of imports that could be brought into the country and required that they be sold at artificially high prices.

In the new system, every aspect of the Egyptian economy was subject to the supervision and control of an extensive bureaucracy headquartered in Alexandria, but with agents—Greek at the upper levels and Egyptian at the lower—in even the most remote village. To facilitate proper functioning of the system, every person from royal peasant to immigrant soldier was registered according to place of residence and economic function. Annually, each village was instructed what crops to plant. Peasants and their animals were forbidden to leave their villages during key phases of the agricultural cycle such as planting and harvesting, and royal officials had first claim on the crop. By Cleopatra's time, even the temples had been brought within the system. Government officials oversaw the management of their lands and revenues, and provided the priests and other temple staff with subsidies to perform their functions and maintain the temple buildings.

HOW DID PTOLEMAIC EGYPT REALLY WORK?

Ptolemy II's goal in developing this system was clearly to bring as much as possible of the Egyptian economy under the supervision and control of the government. While his intentions are clear, the extent of his success is less so. The first historians who studied the Ptolemaic administration of Egypt optimistically described it as a successful example of Greek rational planning applied to the government of an "oriental" kingdom. As scholars have investigated how the system actually worked, however, it has become increasingly clear that the idea of Ptolemaic Egypt as an orderly planned society managed by a rational and efficient bureaucracy is a myth.

The original view had resulted from scholars' efforts to understand the mass of papyri discovered by archeologists, most of which deal with individual transactions such as tax receipts or royal decisions with little if any explanation of why they were created. As a result, scholars devoted particular attention to documents such as the so-called "Revenue Laws of Ptolemy II" and "The Instructions of a Dioiketes [financial administrator] to his Oikonomos [steward]," which seemed to be official handbooks of the rules governing the organization and administration of some of the most important governmental and economic institutions of Ptolemaic Egypt. Moreover, they were encouraged to interpret these documents in this manner based on their similarity to documents issued by the new bureaucracies that developed in late-nineteenth- and twentieth-century Europe and America.

On closer investigation, however, the similarity proved to be superficial. Thus, close analysis revealed that the "Revenue Laws of Ptolemy II" do not describe the actual management of the Ptolemaic oil monopoly but the government's unrealistic idea of how such a monopoly ought to work. Similarly, another document, the so-called "crop planting schedule," which was originally thought to be a plan drawn up annually in Alexandria that set out in detail for each region of Egypt the crops to be planted in the following year, turned out instead to be a report compiled by the central government from speculative assessments by local officials of their district's future crops. Its purpose was not to rationally plan Egyptian agriculture but to provide crude estimates of the government's future revenues. Likewise, "The Instructions of a Dioiketes to his Oikonomos" was not an official manual for new administrators but a literary work describing the duties and character of an ideal official.

The Ptolemaic administration also lacked some of the key characteristics of any true bureaucracy, such as defined career paths, clear chains of command, and clearly specified areas of responsibility for its officials. The problem started at the top and extended throughout the government. While Ptolemaic Egypt was an autocracy, it was a personal autocracy. The government consisted of the king, his friends (the king's personal entourage), and the army. Government officials were not professional civil servants but political appointees, who often had multiple and sometimes even overlapping responsibilities. Nor were they trained for their offices but fulfilled whatever position the king posted them to, irrespective of their previous service. Moreover, not only were they untrained, but—as the practice of selling government papers in bulk to undertakers reveals—they also lacked such basic bureaucratic tools as comprehensive archives to assist them in making their decisions.

In other words, the Ptolemaic administration was far from being a rationally designed and efficient bureaucratic machine intended to manage a complex planned economy. Instead, it was a system riddled with irrationalities and inefficiencies, whose primary purpose was to control the king's Egyptian subjects and to extract the maximum amount of revenue from them. Documents such as the recently discovered Egyptian translation of Ptolemy II's order for a complete economic survey of Egypt, and his letter threatening lawyers—whose support of their clients reduce revenue—with fines and confiscation of their property bear witness to his insatiable need for money to support his ambitious foreign policies.

Not surprisingly, abuse was inherent in the system. From its origins in the reign of Ptolemy II to the time of Cleopatra, rulers found it necessary to repeatedly issue royal orders forbidding government officials from exploiting the king's subjects for personal gain. The situation eventually became so serious that kings routinely began their reign by publishing blanket amnesties forgiving unpaid debts owed the government and canceling outstanding charges of wrongdoing by government officials so as to provide a "clean slate" for the new reign. Equally unsurprising, resistance to the system's demands was also rampant. Resistance took many forms, but the most important was a form of strike that Ptolemaic documents refer to as anachoresis, "withdrawal"—the abandonment *en masse* of their villages and fields by royal peasants. The purpose of anachoresis was not revolution but to pressure local officials to reduce their demands by threatening the revenues on which the government depended, and the ploy often succeeded because maintenance of the revenue stream was more important then enforcing the letter of royal policy. This was true from the origin of the system under Ptolemy II to its end during the reign of Cleopatra, whose decrees forbid the same abuses as those of her great ancestor.

Contemporary historians' views of Ptolemaic Egypt are more complex than those of the scholars who first studied the papyri and tried to reconstruct the Ptolemaic organization of Egypt. On the one hand, there is no doubt that the government was able to extract large revenues from its subjects. Records still available in Alexandria in the second century c.e. revealed that during the reign of Ptolemy II, revenues were sufficient to support a huge military establishment that included 240,000 infantry and cavalry, 300 war elephants, and 3,500 warships.[3] And two centuries later, when Egyptian power had declined from its third-century b.c.e. peak, Cleopatra was still able to conduct a substantial building program, build at least two fleets, and assume much of the cost of Antony's various campaigns. At the same time, however, the repeated references to resistance by the Ptolemies' subjects to the government's demands and the crown's inability to prevent abuses by its own officials make it clear that royal autocracy was more apparent than real. It was only through flexibility and compromise that even the strongest Ptolemies such as Ptolemy II and Cleopatra could achieve their goals.

CHAPTER 4

CLEOPATRA'S EGYPT: A MULTICULTURAL SOCIETY

When Cleopatra died in 30 B.C.E., Macedonian rule in Egypt had lasted for three centuries, the longest period of foreign rule in Egyptian history to that time. One effect of Macedonian rule was a great increase in the number of non-Egyptians in the country. It is reasonable to wonder, therefore, what it meant to be a non-Egyptian—particularly a Greek or Jew—living in Egypt during those centuries. The question has occupied both ancient and modern historians; both have given surprisingly similar answers. It meant being a member of a small colonial elite living in a densely populated—ancient estimates put the population of Ptolemaic Egypt at about seven million people—and exotic land occupied by a people with a millennia-long history and strange customs like animal worship. The reality was more complex. Far from being monolithic, Egyptian society was one of the earliest multicultural societies in history.

At first glance this conclusion is surprising. Egyptian texts sharply distinguish Egypt and Egyptians from all foreign peoples, so we would expect Egyptian society to be closed to non-Egyptians, but that was not the case. In actuality, Egyptian society was simultaneously open and xenophobic. From earliest times, non-Egyptians settled in Egypt and melded into Egyptian society. For much of Egyptian history, acceptance was not difficult, since all that was required was that foreigners accept Egyptian traditions and values. Acculturation was made easier by the fact that for most of Egyptian history, the majority of non-Egyptians who settled in Egypt did so as individuals. As there was no barrier to intermarriage, after a generation or two, immigrants merged into the general population. In the first millennium B.C.E., however, when Greeks and Jews entered Egypt in large numbers, this was no longer the case.

As Egypt came under foreign rule, increasingly individual immigration was replaced by the settlement of whole ethnic groups. Acculturation, which had previously smoothed the entry of foreigners into Egyptian society, functioned less efficiently since the new groups tended to be either Egypt's new rulers or their allies. Such groups had less incentive to lose their ethnic identity since it marked them as different and superior to the Egyptians they ruled. Even peoples like the Libyans and Nubians, who had long histories of contact with Egypt and had been strongly influenced by Egyptian culture, resisted full assimilation. Egyptians, for their part, responded to these developments by heightening their own sense of Egyptianness, emphasizing their past superiority to their new masters, and elaborating those aspects of their culture that were most distinctive, such as the cult of sacred animals. Not surprisingly, ambivalence and tension increasingly characterized relations between Egyptians and non-Egyptians. This was particularly true of relations between Egyptians and Greeks and Jews, who had no such histories and were, therefore, particularly resistant to Egyptianization.

JEWS AND GREEKS IN EGYPT BEFORE ALEXANDER

Jewish and Greek contact with Egypt began long before Alexander's reign. Indeed, according to Jewish tradition preserved in the biblical story of the Exodus, Jews lived in Egypt for several centuries before fleeing the country late in the second millennium B.C.E. Although the Bible provides evidence for diplomatic contact between Egypt and the Jewish kingdoms in the early first millennium B.C.E., it was only in the early seventh century B.C.E. that Jews began to settle in Egypt again. The initial impetus for this renewal of Jewish settlement in Egypt was the reliance of the pharaohs of the 26th dynasty on the support of foreign mercenaries to maintain their control of Egypt and defend its independence against foreign threats.

Jewish mercenaries served in the army of Psamtek II during his Nubian campaign in 593 B.C.E. and continued in Egyptian service until the Persian conquest of Egypt in 525 B.C.E., when they entered Persian service. Although evidence suggests the presence of Jewish soldiers in Memphis and other Egyptian cities during the sixth and fifth centuries B.C.E., only the settlement at Elephantine near the southern border of Egypt is well known, thanks to the discovery of numerous Aramaic papyri that provide detailed evidence about the life of its inhabitants and their rocky relationship with their Egyptian neighbors. Although the evidence points to the continued presence of Jews in Egypt in the fourth century B.C.E., it is unlikely that they continued to enjoy the same privileged position they had had under Persian rule during the period of renewed Egyptian independence that lasted from 404 B.C.E. to 343 B.C.E.

The early history of Greek settlement in Egypt is similar to that of the Jews. Contact between Greeks and Egypt in the late second millennium B.C.E. was followed by several centuries of relative isolation, resuming only in the early seventh century B.C.E. Like the Jews, Greeks first settled in Egypt as mercenaries in the service of the twenty-sixth-dynasty pharaohs. Greek soldiers fought in the army of Psamtek I when he rebelled against Assyrian rule and served along with Jewish soldiers in the Nubian campaign of Psamtek II. Greek garrisons are attested in both Lower and Upper Egypt as well as in a Greek quarter in Memphis. By the late sixth century B.C.E., Egyptian trade with the Aegean was extensive enough for the pharaoh, Amasis, to allow a consortium of twelve Greek cities to found the city of Naukratis in the western Delta, which served as the center for all trade between Greece and Egypt. Unlike the Jews, however, Greeks supported the Egyptians in their efforts to escape Persian rule; consequently, Greek influence in Egypt increased during the period of renewed Egyptian independence in the first half of the fourth century B.C.E.

JEWS AND GREEKS IN PTOLEMAIC EGYPT

The Greek and Jewish settlements existing in Egypt before Alexander's invasion in 332 B.C.E. formed the nucleus of the Greek and Jewish populations in Ptolemaic Egypt. The scale of the Greek and Jewish presence in Egypt, however, expanded greatly under Macedonian rule. The Greeks came first in two waves, one under Alexander and a second and much larger one under the early Ptolemies—particularly Ptolemy II, whose efforts to attract Greeks to Egypt earned him the reputation of being "the best paymaster for a free man."[1] There were also two large waves of Jewish immigration—one under Ptolemy I, consisting largely of

enslaved prisoners captured during Ptolemy's capture of Jerusalem in 307
B.C.E., and a second in the 170s B.C.E., composed of political refugees fleeing the expansion of Seleukid influence in Judaea—supplemented by the
sort of small-scale population movements that had typified relations between Egypt and Palestine for centuries.

Reliable statistics are lacking for Greek and Jewish immigration to
Egypt, but it is likely that by the time of Cleopatra, the total number of
Greeks and Jews in Egypt was close to a million—approximately 14 per-
cent of the population of Egypt. The reason for this extraordinary mi-
gration, one of the largest in ancient history, is not in doubt. While
Alexander seems to have hoped to include members of the old elite of
the Persian Empire in the ruling class of his empire in order to make up
for the limited number of Macedonians available to him, Ptolemy I and
the other successors did not share this vision, preferring instead to enlist
the support of peoples with strong military traditions but who could not
threaten their control of their kingdoms—hence, like Greeks and Jews.

The effects of increased immigration on Egypt and the lives of Egyptians were dramatic. During the reign of Alexander, Egyptians could be
found at all levels of government, and members of the former royal family held high military positions. A generation later, Egyptian soldiers still
made up a large part of Ptolemy I's army. By the reign of Ptolemy II, however, this was no longer true. Greeks monopolized government offices
above the village level, and Egyptians had been largely eliminated from
the military. It was only in desperation that Ptolemy IV reintroduced
Egyptians into the phalanx in the late third century B.C.E. Their place
had been taken by a new class of Greek and Jewish immigrant soldiers
paid with land grants called cleruchies, which were worked by Egyptian
farmers who leased them from the soldiers.

SOCIAL RELATIONS IN PTOLEMAIC EGYPT

The nature of relations between the various ethnic groups in Ptolemaic Egypt is one of the oldest problems in its historiography. Before
analysis of papyri provided insights into how the Ptolemaic system actually worked, historians offered idealized interpretations of Ptolemaic society, viewing it as a "melting pot" in which Greek and non-Greeks
blended into a new cosmopolitan civilization. More recently, a harsher
view has become popular in which interaction between ethnic groups

was minimal, and social status and privilege were determined by ethnicity—with Macedonian and Greek identity ranking highest and Egyptian lowest.

There is a considerable degree of truth in the view of Ptolemaic Egypt as a segregated society thanks to the organization of the kingdom. Certainly, the fact that Cleopatra was the first member of her dynasty to learn to speak Egyptian suggests that relations between the Greek and Macedonian upper class and native Egyptians were limited. Moreover, unlike their Seleukid rivals, the founding of cities, where the two peoples might interact, was not part of the Ptolemies' strategy for governing Egypt. There were only three Greek cities in all of Egypt: Alexandria; the old colony of Naukratis; and Ptolemais, near Thebes in Upper Egypt. As Greek and Jewish settlement was largely confined to these cities and new villages built on reclaimed land in the Fayum, and nome capitals, the reality was that the vast majority of Egyptians who lived in the countryside had little contact with either Greeks or Jews. Not surprisingly, studies of Egyptian villages have revealed an almost total absence of either Greek or Jewish residents or foreign influence on the daily life of their inhabitants.

Social segregation existed in the cities also. Egyptians were not citizens of the three Greek cities. They lived in separate residential quarters and intermarriage was forbidden. The Ptolemies even maintained separate legal systems for their Greek, Jewish, and Egyptian subjects. Tension between these groups was inevitable, and evidence documenting that fact is found throughout Ptolemaic history.

The evidence is fullest for relations between Greeks and Egyptians. Thus, the third century B.C.E. poet Theokritos characterizes petty street crime as "mugging Egyptian style,"[2] while an Egyptian in the service of a government official complains that his Greek supervisors hold him in contempt and have refused to pay him for months "because I am a barbarian." A century later the personal papers of a Greek recluse living in the temple of Sarapis at Memphis are filled with references to incidents of personal harassment by his Egyptian neighbors. Complaints of assaults on Greeks by Egyptians or disrespect of Greeks are not uncommon in legal documents.

Tension between Egyptians and Jews is also attested, but unlike the situation with the Greeks, it was ideological in origin. The primary source of the hostility was the Exodus story and the sacrifice of the paschal lamb during the Passover festival, both of which Egyptians found deeply offensive. Already in the fifth century B.C.E. priests of the creator god Khnum to whom lambs were sacred instigated attacks on the Jews at Elephantine and their temple. Similar violence is not known to have occurred in Ptolemaic Egypt, but the historian Manetho and other Egyptian writers produced antisemitic versions of the Exodus story. In these versions of the story, Jews were portrayed not as an enslaved people seeking their freedom but as lepers and impious criminals expelled by a pious pharaoh to purify Egypt. Even more hostile is an anonymous prophecy extant in a third century C.E. text but probably dating to the second century B.C.E. that urges Egyptians to attack the Jews or "your city will become desolate."[3]

It is understandable that many Egyptians longed for the return of native rule and that prophecy of the end of Macedonian rule is a common theme in Hellenistic Egyptian literature. Two such texts still survive. The one known as the *Prophecy of the Lamb* held out the hope of the return of native Egyptian rule but only after nine hundred years of brutal foreign rule,[4] while the *Potter's Oracle* more optimistically claimed that the Greeks and Macedonians would turn on each other and open the way for a savior king to free Egypt. Some Egyptians went further and identified the royal savior with a son of Nektanebo II, the last pharaoh of a free Egypt, who had fled to Nubia when the Persians reconquered Egypt in the 340s B.C.E. but would return some day to free Egypt.

It is equally understandable that not all Egyptians were content to wait for the miraculous appearance of a savior king. In the 240s B.C.E., a native revolt forced Ptolemy III to abandon his invasion of the Seleukid kingdom and return to Egypt. The Rosetta stone, which enabled scholars to decipher hieroglyphic writing, commemorates the suppression of another such rebellion in the first years of the reign of Ptolemy V. The greatest such uprising, however, broke out in 207/6 B.C.E., and for almost two decades, native pharaohs ruled Upper Egypt before the rebellion was crushed by the forces of Ptolemy V. During this last rebellion, the city of Thebes regained for the last time its centuries-old glory as the capital of an Egyptian kingdom, and its chief god Amon was again the patron of a pharaoh, while Egyptian documents ignored the Ptolemies and their divine protectors.

Nevertheless, the description of Ptolemaic Egypt as a rigidly segregated society polarized between oppressive non-Egyptians and rebellious Egyptians is as much an oversimplification as the idea that it was the home of a harmoniously mixed Hellenistic civilization. The existence of Greek translations of Egyptian texts such as "The Dream of Nekitanebos" indicates that some Greeks were interested in contemporary Egyptian culture, while the claim that Alexander was really the son of Nektanebo II and the hoped-for savior king equally proves that some Egyptians were prepared to accept Macedonian rule. The reality was that social divisions and conflicts within Egyptian society made unified resistance to Macedonian rule impossible.

For millennia, the security of Egypt and its kings depended on the support of the gods and their priesthoods, and that remained true of Ptolemaic Egypt. One of the principal sources of Egyptian discontent under Persian rule had been the Persians' niggardliness toward the temples and hostility toward the cult of sacred animals such as the Apis bull. Alexander and the Ptolemies after him strove to avoid the Persians' mistakes. Thus, although the Ptolemies subjected the temples of Egypt to greater supervision than their pharaonic predecessors, they also maintained and expanded the scale of state subsidy of religion. Thus, the Ptolemies participated in the cult of the Apis and Buchis bulls and underwrote the costs of their burials. They also built temples for the Egyptian gods on a scale that had not been seen since the height of the new kingdom a thousand years earlier. Indeed, many of the temples that tourists visit today were built by the Ptolemies and not their pharaonic predecessors.

Egyptian evidence suggests that the Ptolemies' policies worked and won them considerable support among the Egyptian religious elite. Priestly families prospered, accumulating large estates and actively engaging in business transactions of all kinds, while expending large sums on the traditional Egyptian indicators of personal success: dedications to the gods and lavish tomb furnishings. Their prosperity also provided the basis for a vigorous revival of Egyptian culture, resulting in a variety of new and interesting literary and artistic works that are only now being studied and appreciated. It is not surprising, therefore, that native rebellions targeted both priests and major Ptolemaic temples—such as that at Edfu—or that in the Rosetta stone, Ptolemy V is congratulated for his brutal suppression of a native rebellion at Lykopolis in Lower Egypt that threatened the welfare of the Egyptian priesthood just as much as it did their Macedonian overlord.

Opportunities to acquire wealth were not limited to the religious elite. Analysis of the personal archives of village officials such as Menches, the village scribe of Kerkeosiris, has revealed that such people could grow rich by exploiting their role as essential intermediaries between the Greek-speaking central government and its Egyptian subjects. Not surprisingly, local officials were loyal supporters of the Ptolemaic regime, and were also singled out for reprisal during native uprisings in the late third and second centuries B.C.E.

While religious differences reinforced the mutual isolation of Jews and Egyptians, social and cultural factors tended to moderate the segregation of Greeks and Egyptians in Ptolemaic Egypt. The most important of these factors was demography. At the beginning of the Hellenistic period, intermarriage between Greeks and Egyptians was relatively common, since the majority of Greek immigrants were soldiers and, therefore, predominantly male. Understandably, the few Greek women, who immigrated into Egypt, were highly valued. Marriage contracts and letters preserved among the papyri reveal that, unlike women in Greece, they could petition the government in their own name and even initiate divorce proceedings if their husbands humiliated them or were unfaithful. Nevertheless, although the Ptolemies actively encouraged Greek immigration with generous rewards, the total number of immigrants was relatively small, and the majority of those came in the early years of Macedonian rule. By the second century B.C.E., Greek immigration had largely stopped. The number of ethnic Greeks in Ptolemaic Egypt was, therefore, probably small.

Equally, except for the inhabitants of Alexandria, Naukratis, and Ptolemais, most Greek immigrants lived in predominantly Egyptian environments where intermarriage was not uncommon, and few of the traditional political or social institutions of Greek culture existed. For all intents and purposes, therefore, the majority of Greeks in Egypt remained essentially resident aliens who retained the citizenship of their home poleis, as can be seen from the fact that Egyptian Greeks continued to identify themselves by their *poleis* of origin in public and private documents even after their families had resided in Egypt for several generations. Greeks living in such circumstances tended to assimilate to the social and cultural mores of their non-Greek neighbors and inlaws. A good example of the result of such assimilation is the family of a Greek cavalry officer named Dryton, whose wife and children all have Egyptian names and used both Greek and Egyptian indiscriminately in their business and legal activities but proudly considered themselves Greek. The results of this process of assimilation are most visible, however, in the area of religion, since Greeks, like other polytheists, were already predisposed to honor the gods of countries in which they lived.

RELIGION IN PTOLEMAIC EGYPT

In Ptolemaic Egypt, a Hellenized form of Egyptian religion developed as some of the old *polis* gods came to appear anachronistic or irrelevant to the country's Greek population. The most striking product of this Hellenized Egyptian religion was to be found in Alexandria, where Ptolemy I called on the Egyptian priest and historian Manetho and the Athenian ritual expert Timotheos to create a new god to serve as the city's new patron deity. The new god, Sarapis, was a synthesis of Egyptian and Greek elements, combining aspects of Hades, Osiris, Asklepios, and Zeus. Outside Alexandria, Greeks worshiped traditional Egyptian gods such as Isis and Osiris. The centuries-old Greek practice of identifying their own gods with those of other peoples (syncretism) encouraged acceptance of these strange deities, but the process of identification itself entailed losses as well as gains.

Native Egyptian practices that too obviously conflicted with Greek religious traditions, such as animal worship or mummification, were purged from the new Hellenized cults, while the Egyptian gods took on the identities of the Greek gods with whom they were identified. The result is evident in the case of Isis. Originally the devoted wife of Osiris and mother of Horus in the charter myth of the Egyptian monarchy, Isis, through her identification with Greek goddesses such as Aphrodite, Demeter, and Athena, assumed a character unprecedented in Egyptian tradition: queen of the universe, benefactress of all people, and creator of civilization. When accommodation between Greek and non-Greek culture occurred, therefore, it occurred in such a way that the result did not challenge the dominance of Greek culture and values. As a result of these developments, the worship of Isis spread widely not only among the non-Egyptian population of Ptolemaic Egypt but also outside Egypt after the Roman conquest, when it became one of the chief rivals to Christianity.

The implications of these developments for understanding the nature of Egyptian society in Cleopatra's Egypt are profound. When her ancestor Ptolemy I became king in 305 B.C.E., Greeks living in Egypt were either immigrants or the descendants of immigrants from the Greek cities of the Aegean. By the time of Cleopatra, however, this was not true. No longer were Greeks necessarily members of a particular ethnic group but persons who her government said were Greek.

As the Ptolemaic government recognized only two kinds of people in Egypt—native Egyptians and Greeks—and distinguished them according to whether they used the Greek or Egyptian legal system, this meant that the privileged class of Greeks had expanded to include all persons of Greek culture. Greeks in Cleopatra's Egypt, therefore, were people who spoke Greek and who had received a Greek education, adopted a Greek lifestyle (and frequently a Greek name), and worshiped their old gods under Greek names. Greek-educated Egyptians as well as the children of mixed marriages qualified under this rule. Even Jews could sometimes be classified as Greeks—despite the religious differences separating them from other "Greeks"—if they were Greek speakers and used the Greek legal system.[5]

These developments were mutually beneficial for wealthy non-Greeks and the Ptolemaic state. For ambitious individuals, the value of being considered a Greek was considerable. Not only did they become eligible for high-ranking government jobs and contracts, but they paid lower taxes than Egyptians and were exempt from humiliating punishments such a being publicly whipped. It is not surprising, therefore, that upper class Egyptians and Jews sought Greek identification and the Greek education that made it possible. The benefit to the Ptolemaic state is equally clear. The Greek population of Egypt continued to expand after Aegean immigration dried up in the late third century B.C.E. Equally important, their acceptance as Greeks tended to alienate those who received such identification from the bulk of the native Egyptian population, thereby reducing the number of potential leaders for movements hostile to the Ptolemies. As a result, the increasing interaction of the Greek and non-Greek populations of second and first century B.C.E. Egypt—which Aegean Greeks and Romans condemned—far from leading to the ruin of Ptolemaic Egypt actually contributed to its survival.

CHAPTER 5

ALEXANDRIA: CITY OF CULTURE AND CONFLICT

BIRTH OF A CITY

The fate of rulers and cities are often closely connected. Thus, the fifth century B.C.E. statesman Perikles and the Roman emperor Augustus are inextricably linked with Athens and Rome. Similarly, Cleopatra VII is tightly connected to the city of Alexandria, where she spent most of her life and where many of the most famous events of her reign took place.

Located near the mouth of the Canopic branch of the Nile at the western edge of the delta, Alexandria was the first, most famous, and most enduring of Alexander's many city foundations. Alexander founded the city on the site of a small Egyptian town named Rhakotis just before leaving Egypt in the spring of 331 B.C.E. His motives for choosing this particular site were probably mixed. Located at one of the few good harbors in the Delta and possessing easy access to the Nile and the interior of Egypt, Alexandria was ideally situated to replace the nearby Greek city of Naukratis as the principal link between Egypt and Greece. Alexander's interest in the site, however, was also sparked by the fact that just offshore lay the island of Pharos, the site of one of the most famous episodes in the works of his beloved Homer—the struggle between Menelaos and the shape-shifting wizard Proteus in the *Odyssey*.

Alexandria occupied a unique place in the Hellenistic world. Although it was built around an existing Egyptian settlement and functioned as the capital of Egypt, Alexandria was not itself officially part of Egypt. It was, instead, a Greek city-state with its own territory, as its ancient name "Alexandria by Egypt" indicates. As in any Greek city-state, Alexandrian citizenship was limited to the Greeks and Macedonians whom Alexander and the Ptolemies encouraged to settle in the new city. These groups, however, formed only a small portion of Alexandria's total population. A liberal immigration policy created a multiethnic population including Egyptians, Syrians, and Nubians, as well as a vibrant Jewish community that eventually occupied fully one-fifth of the city's area and whose great synagogue was considered second only to the temple in Jerusalem as one of the marvels of the Jewish world.

Alexandria flourished as a result of the patronage of the Ptolemies and its dual role of capital of Egypt and commercial link between the Mediterranean and Africa, Arabia, and the countries bordering the Indian Ocean. By the time Cleopatra came to the throne in 50 B.C.E., Alexandria had grown to a city of more than 500,000 inhabitants and was the premier city of the Mediterranean basin.

ALEXANDRIA: THE CITY

Although Alexander only had time during his stay in Egypt to lay out the general outlines of Alexandria, his plans were on a grand scale. The city was planned as a rectangle divided into four quarters by two wide boulevards that intersected at its center. He also ordered the building of a mole almost a mile long to connect Pharos to the mainland, thereby creating two sheltered harbors. Responsibility for embellishing the city, however, fell to the Ptolemies, who in the words of the geographer Strabo built "many fine public precincts and palaces, which occupy a fourth or even a third of the city's whole perimeter; for just as each of the kings added some adornment to its public monuments, so each added his own residence to those already existing."

Perhaps the clearest symbol of the dynamism and originality of Alexandria, however, was its signature monument, the Pharos lighthouse, which was considered one of the Seven Wonders of the Ancient World and whose fame even reached China.[1] The Pharos lighthouse was built by the architect Sostratus of Knidos for Ptolemy II and was the world's first skyscraper. Containing three stages, its polygonal tower rose over three hundred feet above Alexandria and was topped by a statue of Zeus Soter (savior), whose beacon fire was visible far out to sea and guided ships to Alexandria.

Today little remains of Alexandria's ancient splendor on the ground. An earthquake toppled the lighthouse into the sea in the fourteenth century C.E., while continuous occupation of the site has eliminated virually all remains of ancient Alexandria, allowing scholars to speculate that ancient visitors would have encountered a purely Greek city. As is its wont, however, archaeology has revolutionized our understanding of Cleopatra's and her predecessor's Alexandria.

As a result of tectonic changes in the Mediterranean since antiquity, the sea has encroached on much of the shoreline of ancient Alexandria and its suburbs. Thus, while little of the ancient city survives within modern Alexandria, much of the ancient royal quarter of Alexandria lies submerged in the shallow waters of Alexandria harbor. Underwater archaeologists began exploring this treasure in the 1990s and discovered not only the remains of Greek-style buildings and sculpture but also large amounts of Egyptian sculpture, which the Ptolemies had brought to their capital from all over Egypt. Instead of a purely Greek city, the Ptolemies had created an urban setting in which both Egyptian and Greek aspects of their kingdom were celebrated, providing a dramatic setting for the city's cultural and political life.

CITY OF CULTURE

The Ptolemies strove to make Alexandria the cultural center of the Greek world. Like Alexander—whose entourage had included artists and intellectuals such as Aristotle's nephew, Kallisthenes, his court historian—Ptolemy I and his immediate successors encouraged prominent Greek scholars and scientists to come to Egypt. With the enormous wealth of Egypt at their disposal, the Ptolemies could afford to subsidize intellectuals, encouraging artistic and scientific work by establishing cultural institutions of a new type.

Their principal cultural foundation was the Museum, which received its name because it was organized as a temple dedicated to the nine Muses, the patron goddesses of the arts. Because the Museum was organized as a religious institution, its director was a priest of the Muses appointed by the government. The model for the Museum was the Peripatos, the school Aristotle founded in Athens in the late 330s B.C.E. Like the Peripatos, the Museum was not a teaching institution but a research center containing gardens and residential quarters, where distinguished scholars, intellectuals, and technicians could pursue their studies in congenial surroundings.

The Museum's grounds included dormitories, dining facilities, and pleasant gardens in which its members could meet and talk about their projects. Like its director, the members of the Museum were appointed by the government and received stipends to enable them to devote their energies to their work. One envious rival sneered at the successful occupants of Ptolemy's "bird coop" with some justification, since subsidized intellectuals were expected to earn their keep. Doctors and writers receiving government stipends served as physicians and tutors to members of the royal family, and celebrated its achievements. Thus, in his poem *The Lock of Berenice*, the third-century B.C.E. scholar and poet Kallimakhos described the transformation into a comet of a lock of hair dedicated by Berenice II in 246 BC to commemorate the beginning of the Third Syrian War. In a similar vein, Theokritos' seventeenth *Idyll* extravagantly praised the first decade of Ptolemy II's reign.

Closely connected to the Museum was the famous Alexandrian Library, which Ptolemy I established with the aid and advice of Demetrios of Phaleron—an Athenian politician and student of Aristotle, who was living in exile in Egypt. Like the Museum, the Library was not open to the public but was intended to assist the members of the Museum in pursuing their studies. To that end, it was meant to contain copies of every book written in Greek. By the time of Cleopatra, the Library is estimated to have contained 700,000 papyrus rolls in its collection.

The Ptolemies' passion for expanding the royal Library's collections was legendary. The Greek translation of the Jewish Bible, the *Septuagint*, was supposedly produced on order of Ptolemy II, and the official Athenian copy of the works of the three canonical tragedians was allegedly stolen by Ptolemy III. Even the books of visitors to Egypt were scrutinized and seized—the owner receiving a cheap copy as a replacement—if they were not part of the Library's collection. However its books were acquired, the Library offered unprecedented resources for scholarly research in every field of intellectual endeavor, provided, of course, they were reliable copies.

Already in antiquity there were rumors that unscrupulous book dealers provided the Ptolemies with forged copies of unknown letters and works by famous Greek writers. Kallimakhos began the process of authenticating the Library's holdings by creating a monumental catalogue of the Library in 120 books that laid the foundation for the history of Greek literature. Later scholars and librarians concentrated their efforts on identifying the authentic works of the major Greek writers including Homer, the lyric poets, the Athenian tragedians, and orators.

Although the goal of Kallimakhos and his successors—and the rulers who supported them—was to produce reliable texts of the works of major Greek writers for the Alexandrian Library, their work quickly gained an audience beyond the walls of the Museum and Library. How this happened is not known in detail, but a growing book trade catering to both Greeks and non-Greeks who desired to acquire a Greek education was certainly a factor. In any event, study of papyrus copies of Greek literary works has revealed that within a few hundred years of the establishment of the Museum and Library, the texts of the works of the major authors had been standardized in forms that are the ancestors of the versions we still read today.

Alexandrian Literature

The work of Alexandrian intellectuals was not limited, however, to satisfying the whims of their royal patrons. Alexandrian writers made important innovations in Greek literature. In his *Idylls*—brief dialogues or monologues set in an idealized countryside—Theokritos introduced the pastoral mode into western literature. Kallimakhos inaugurated the tradition of "learned" poetry in works such as his *Hymns* and *Aetia*, in which he retold in elegant verse obscure myths and the origins of strange customs and festivals collected from all over the Greek world. Kallimakhos' younger contemporary and rival the librarian Apollonios of Rhodes reinvigorated the old epic genre with his acute psychological portraits of Jason and Medea in his vivid retelling of the story of Jason and the Argonauts, the *Argonautica*. Another contemporary of Kallimakhos—Euhemeros, an ambassador of Cassander to Ptolemy I—put forward a radical and important theory about the origins of mythology: he invented the utopian travel romance in order to propound in his *Sacred Tale* the notion that the gods were great rulers worshiped after their deaths for their gifts to humanity.

The literary language of Ptolemaic Alexandria was Greek, but the creation of literary texts was not limited to Greeks; instead, it was multicultural like the city's population. The most active of the city's other ethnic groups was Alexandria's large Jewish community. The most important Jewish work produced in Ptolemaic Alexandria was the Greek translation of the Old Testament known as the *Septuagint* (version of the seventy). Pious legend claimed that it was created by seventy divinely in-spired translators at the instigation of Ptolemy II, who wished to include a copy of the Jewish scriptures in the Library; in actuality, it took almost two centuries to complete the translation. Its importance, however, can-not be overestimated, since it was the existence of the *Septuagint* that made possible the spread of Christianity in the Roman Empire.

The *Septuagint* was not, however, the only literary work produced by Jewish writers living in Alexandria. They also wrote epic poems, dramas, histories, and short stories using themes drawn from the Bible. Although only fragments of these works survive, we can see that two themes char-acterized them: the need to provide Jewish readers with religiously ap-propriate reading material that was comparable to pagan Greek literature and the desire to rebut Greek and Egyptian claims that Jews had not played an important role in the development of civilization. Some Jew-ish writers went even further in their attempt to find a bridge between Jewish and Greek thought. Thus, the philosopher Aristoboulos argued in a work addressed to Ptolemy VI that the god of the Jews and the Greek philosophers were the same, and that Plato and other Greek philosophers were influenced by the ideas of Moses in developing their ideas—a the-ory that early Christian thinkers would use later to justify the preserva-tion of pagan literature.

The Jews were not the only non-Greek writers in Alexandria. There were also Egyptian writers, who similarly tried to emphasize the great role Egypt had played in history. The most famous of these Egyptian writers was the priest Manetho, who had helped Ptolemy I create the god Sara-pis. Manetho's most famous and important work was a history of Egypt in three books based on Egyptian temple records. Unfortunately, most of Manetho's history is lost, but his list of the Egyptian kings survives and is still used by Egyptologists today. Another important Egyptian writer is the anonymous author of a romantic biography of Alexander the Great known as the *Alexander Romance*, in which Alexander fights monsters and has other fantastic adventures. The author also claims to reveal the truth about Alexander's birth. According to this author, Alexander was not a Macedonian but an Egyptian and the son of Nektanebo II, the last king of Egypt, who deceived his mother Olympias with his magic into believing that she was having intercourse with Philip II of Macedon. This version of Alexander's birth had little influence in antiquity, but in the

Middle Ages it became widely known throughout Eurasia as a result of the *Alexander Romance* being translated into numerous languages, including Persian, Arabic, Hebrew, and Latin.

Scholarship and Science

The greatest achievements of Hellenistic intellectuals, however, were in the areas of literary scholarship and applied science. Although few of their works survive in their original form, their discoveries and achievements were incorporated into the works of later scholars and provided the foundation for much of European and Islamic intellectual activity until the scientific revolution. Thus, in addition to founding the critical study of Greek literature and preparing standard texts of Homer and numerous other writers, Alexandrian scholars prepared essential tools for studying and teaching, including the first Greek grammars, dictionaries, and scholia—that is, notes accompanying a text that explained unusual words and historical and literary allusions found in it.

Important advances were also made in geography and mechanics. The third century B.C.E. librarian and royal tutor Eratosthenes of Kyrene established the principles of scientific cartography, creating the first relatively accurate map of the world known to the Greeks, and produced a strikingly accurate estimate of the circumference of the earth by applying basic principles of plane geometry to evidence he found in explorers' reports contained in the Library. About the same time, the physicist Ktesibios pioneered the study of ballistics and the use of compressed air as a source of power for various types of machines, including musical instruments and weapons such as repeating crossbows. Other scientists experimented with the use of steam power, creating the prototype for a simple steam engine and a device to automatically open the doors of small religious shrines. These studies also found practical applications. Thus, an unknown Ptolemaic technician invented the saqqiyah, an animal-powered waterwheel that is still used today in Egypt and the Sudan, while the application of principles of hydrology enabled Ptolemy II to build a canal linking the Nile to the Red Sea—the ancestor of the modern Suez Canal.

Equally important advances were made in medicine, particularly by the two third century B.C.E. doctors Herophilos and Erasistratos. They made fundamental discoveries concerning the anatomy and functions of the human nervous, circulatory, optical, reproductive, and digestive systems by dissecting corpses, and even vivisecting criminals whom the government provided for the advancement of science. Alexandria also offered them opportunities for profitable collaboration with Egyptian and other non-Greek doctors. Herophilos applied the Egyptian discovery of the pulse to diagnosis and prognosis of fevers by recognizing that the pulse rate was also the heart rate and developing a technique for timing it with a water clock. He also introduced numerous drugs already in use in Egypt and elsewhere in the territories conquered by Alexander into the Greek pharmocopia. Although the heyday of Alexandrian medicine was the third century B.C.E., Alexandria remained an important center of medical activity and instruction throughout the Hellenistic period and beyond. Cleopatra's court physician even produced the earliest known detailed description of bubonic plague.

The importance of royal patronage in Ptolemaic cultural activity did, however, have a drawback. Areas that did not receive royal largess tended to stagnate. Thus, apart from the works of the mathematician Euclid, whose *Elements* was still used to introduce students to geometry in the early twentieth century, the Alexandrian contribution to the theoretical sciences and philosophy, which were of limited interest to the Ptolemies, was undistinguished in quality and limited in quantity.

CITY OF CONFLICT

Modern historians view Alexandria primarily as the capital of Egypt and as a cosmopolitan center of commerce and culture. Ancient scholars agreed but they also emphasized the turbulence of its population and its potential for violence. Examples are numerous, but perhaps the clearest statement of this negative view of Alexandria and its inhabitants is that of the second century B.C.E. historian Polybius,[2] who observed that "the savagery of the inhabitants of Egypt is terrible when their passions are arroused."

The earliest known example of this violence occurred in 204 B.C.E. when the Alexandrians rose in support of the boy king Ptolemy V after the death of his father, Ptolemy IV. When the rioting finally ceased, the clique that had ruled Egypt in the name of Ptolemy IV was dead, having been literally torn apart in the city's stadium, and Ptolemy V was king. Similar cataclysms occurred throughout the rest of Ptolemaic history.

Thus, the populace drove out Ptolemy IX at the instigation of his mother, Cleopatra III, and killed Ptolemy XI after the death of Cleopatra Berenike III; and, of course, they forced Ptolemy XII into exile and almost defeated Julius Caesar and destroyed Cleopatra's dreams of power.

Ancient explanations of the volatility of the Alexandrians focused on the negative effects of living in Egypt with some justification, since the crowded conditions in which the populace lived combined with the tensions between the various ethnic groups living in the city lowered the threshold for public unrest. It was the peculiar political situation created by Alexandria's role as capital of Egypt, however, that repeatedly sparked riots as the various court factions sought to build popular support for their goals. In this political game, the kings courted the Alexandrians by providing spectacles and festivals and benefactions such as gifts and free food in times of shortage, while other groups played on the populace's prejudices to advance their goals. Thus, the murder of the popular queen mother Arsinoe III set off the riots that accompanied the accession of Ptolemy V, while Ptolemy XII's and Cleopatra's enemies exploited the Alexandrians' hatred of the Romans in their bid for power.

Just as the death of Cleopatra VII and the end of the Ptolemaic dynasty did not end Alexandria's role as a commercial and cultural center, this political dynamic survived the Roman conquest. Riots as fierce as any during the reign of the Ptolemies punctuate the history of Roman Egypt, reaching their climax in 391 c.e. when the Christian bishop Theophilos incited the Alexandrians to destroy the Serapeum—the great complex of temples and catacombs where the cult of Serapis had its home—and its library, the greatest surviving monument of the city's pagan past.

CHAPTER 6

CONCLUSION: QUEEN AND SYMBOL

A remarkable period in Egyptian and world history ended with Cleopatra VII's suicide in 30 B.C.E. Cleopatra was the last and, in many ways, the most remarkable of the successors of Alexander the Great. For two decades she struggled to maintain the independence of Egypt and to restore it to the greatness it had enjoyed under her third-century B.C.E. ancestors, and to a remarkable extent she succeeded. Until recently, however, historians have rarely treated Cleopatra as a historical actor with coherent and potentially achievable policies and goals. Instead the emphasis has been on her as a woman trying to act like a man—a woman consumed by ambition who used her sexuality to manipulate Caesar and Antony, ultimately corrupting them and destroying her kingdom in the process.

Yet the evidence presented in this book tells a different story. Although Cleopatra's sexuality and her willingness to use it in pursuit of her goals were real, the truth was that she played three roles in her life—lover, mother, and queen—and the last two were the most important. Despite the claims of her unbridled licentiousness that supposedly even extended to her slaves, she actually had relationships with only two men, Caesar and Antony, and she was, as far as we can tell, faithful to both. She was similarly faithful to her children and to Egypt.

THE QUEEN

Alexander's conquest of Egypt in 332 B.C.E. had been part of a larger process that extended Macedonian rule and Greek culture over the whole of the area from the Mediterranean Sea to western India. Within a century, however, the area of Greco-Macedonian influence had begun to shrink as new powers—most notably Rome in the west and Parthia in the east—emerged on the historical scene. By 50 B.C.E., only Ptolemaic Egypt survived among the successor states of Alexander's empire.

Although Egypt had survived, the kingdom Cleopatra inherited had been greatly weakened. Stripped of its external possessions, wracked by almost chronic dynastic strife, and nearly bankrupt, Egypt was a tempting prize for ambitious Roman politicians. From the moment of her accession in 50 B.C.E., Cleopatra struggled to reverse Egypt's decline, and she enjoyed considerable success. But while Egypt's bleak prospects brightened considerably during her reign, Cleopatra was realistic enough to realize that maintaining complete independence from Rome was not possible. Ensuring the security of Egypt by making it indispensable to the success of Roman plans in the eastern Mediterranean was possible, however, and her efforts throughout her reign were intended to achieve that goal.

Cleopatra's alliances with Julius Caesar and Mark Antony brought temporary relief from the threat of Roman annexation and restoration to Egyptian authority of much of the empire of her ancestors. She also restored stability to the kingdom's internal life. Her admittedly ruthless victory over her siblings in the struggle for the throne and the proclamation of Caesarion as pharaoh raised the possibility of a peaceful succession for the first time in almost a century. Able administration also restored Egypt's economic strength to the point that Cleopatra was able to finance Antony's Parthian expedition and much of the final struggle with Octavian. Even after her death, Egypt's remaining wealth was still great enough to enable Octavian to carry through many of his reforms at Rome without having to resort to the sort of brutal measures that had characterized the reign of the dictator Sulla and the Second Triumvirate.

While Cleopatra's goals for Egypt were realistic, they also represented a gamble with high stakes. They were achievable but beyond the power of Egypt alone. Her father's experience had taught her that success was impossible without the support of Roman patrons and protectors, and in that she was unlucky. She gained recognition for her claim to the throne and the coveted status of friend of the Roman people in 46 B.C.E. from Julius Caesar, only to be threatened with loss of both as a result of his assassination less than two years later. Similarly, the renewal of civil war in 43 B.C.E. forced her to choose a new patron from the members of the

Second Triumvirate. Calculation, propinquity, and Octavian's unremitting hostility to Caesarion combined to make Antony the obvious choice. The failure of Antony's Parthian and Actian campaigns, however, sealed her fate and that of Egypt as well. For the rest of antiquity, Egypt would be a province of the Roman Empire. Although Octavian and his successors were acclaimed as pharaohs, no Roman emperors would rule there and few even visited Egypt.

THE SYMBOL

With the stakes so high and the consequences so great, it is not surprising that the historical Cleopatra was quickly replaced by the symbol. Octavian allowed her to be buried in royal style with Antony and permitted her statues to survive in return for a bribe from one of her friends. Even more remarkable, her Egyptian cult—alone of the Ptolemies—survived well into late antiquity. In the end, however, Romans and not Egyptians created the image of Cleopatra, which powerfully influenced writing about her for the next two millennia.

The Roman image of Cleopatra originated in the virulent propaganda campaign Octavian mounted against her as part of his preparation for his war against Antony. Octavian's motives in developing his propaganda campaign were tactical. Rome had endured decades of civil war. As a result, he had at all costs to avoid conveying the impression that his struggle with Antony meant that Romans were to fight Romans yet again, especially since Antony still commanded a wide following in Italy. His solution was to ignore Antony and focus Roman suspicion and hostility on Cleopatra instead.

The best propaganda is the simplest and that was true of Octavian's. Two themes dominated it. First, Antony was no longer master of his destiny but was totally subservient to Cleopatra. She had used sex to entrap him and lure him away from the beneficent influence of his wife Octavia. Now, she was forcing him to act against Rome, giving her and her children territories belonging to the Roman people and raising armies to invade Italy. Second and even worse, Cleopatra's goal was not the welfare of Egypt but the subjection of Rome to Egypt through the use of her tool, Antony.

As Octavian defined the meaning of the conflict, what was at stake was nothing less than the survival of Italian culture and values. Should

Cleopatra's "evil" plans succeed and were she to give orders from the Capitol as she was supposed to have desired, Romans would "degenerate into Egyptians"[1] just as had happened to the Macedonians. Fortunately, Romans were told, she failed. Octavian's "glorious victory" at the Battle of Actium and Cleopatra's and Antony's subsequent deaths ended the "threat." The propaganda offensive against her not only continued after her death but intensified. It had, however, a new focus and character. Instead of an immediate enemy to be defeated, Cleopatra was transformed into a symbol of all the forces that threatened Octavian's new order.

The transformation began immediately after Cleopatra's death. As the ruler of Egypt, Octavian had to define his attitude to his new realm. Although he had granted her request to be buried in royal style with Antony, he openly asserted the superiority of Roman values and traditions to those of Cleopatra and the Ptolemies. So, according to the third-century C.E. Roman historian Cassius Dio,[2] when Octavian visited the tomb of Alexander, he ignored the tombs of the Ptolemies because he "wished to see a king, not corpses"; and he similarly refused to visit the Apis bull because "he was accustomed to worship gods, not cattle." Finally, while priests assigned him the traditional titles of a pharaoh and he was depicted in pharaonic regalia sacrificing to the gods on the walls of Egyptian temples, he refused to be crowned according to Egyptian tradition.

Octavian also quickly put the new image of Cleopatra on display when he returned to Rome in 29 B.C.E. As Julius Caesar had done in 46 B.C.E., Octavian celebrated his conquest of Egypt with a spectacular triumph at Rome. Cleopatra's suicide deprived him of the opportunity to lead her into the city in chains. She was present symbolically, however, in the form of a tableau, which depicted for the first time the story that she died from the bite of a cobra, and her children by Antony did march in the procession. Shortly afterward, Octavian built a great monument on the site of his military camp at the new city of Nicopolis (victory city) to commemorate forever his defeat of the threat to Rome posed by Cleopatra and Antony. Reliefs sculpted with scenes from his triumph decorated it and the bronze rams of the thirty-six ships his forces captured in the battle were mounted on a huge wall two hundred feet long. Coins with the motto *Aegypta capta*—"Egypt has been taken captive"— depicting Octavian's head on the obverse and typical Egyptian symbols such as a crocodile on the reverse spread the message throughout the empire.

The miracle was that Octavian's propaganda also inspired great literature. In the ideology of late-first-century B.C.E. Rome, the Battle of Actium marked the end of the era of the Roman civil wars and the return of peace. Not surprisingly, the battle was celebrated by most of the writers patronized by the emperor Augustus. The main themes already appear in the early 20s B.C.E. in the works of the poet Horace and reappear in the other great Augustan writers. As in the prewar propaganda, the Augustan writers portrayed Antony as little more than Cleopatra's tool, whose fate was sealed the moment he met her. In his monumental history of Rome, the historian Livy explained every misstep of Antony's final years as motivated by his mad love for Cleopatra.

Cleopatra by contrast acquired a kind of grandeur, becoming a worthy foe for Octavian to defeat. She was portrayed as an enemy on the grand scale, one as dangerous as any in Roman history, consumed by her lust and driven by her ambition to rule Rome. In the words of the poet Propertius, "the harlot queen of licentious Canopus, the one disgrace branded on Philip's line, dared to pit barking Anubis against our Jupiter and to force the Tiber to endure the threats of the Nile." Her victory would have meant the end of all that Rome had achieved. Again Propertius: "What profit now is it to have broken the axes of that Tarquin whose proud life gave him a title derived from it, had we been fated to bear a woman's yoke?" When her plans failed, she faced death like a hero. The poet Horace marveled that Cleopatra, faced with the certainty of a humiliating death after marching in Octavian's triumph, "dared even to gaze with serene face upon her fallen palace, courageous, too, to handle poisonous asps, that she might draw black venom to her heart."[3]

Following Octavian's lead, the great Augustan writers set the agenda for later accounts of Cleopatra, but repetition smoothed out the complexity of their picture. The second C.E. biographer Plutarch still provided a well-rounded portrait of the queen in his *Life of Antony*, but he was an exception. Most ignored the heroic aspects of the Augustan picture, even blaming her cowardice for Antony's defeat at Actium. What resulted were accounts reduced largely to increasingly vituperative references to her sexuality and greed. So the mid-first-century C.E. poet Lucan described her in the *Pharsalia*, his historical epic on the civil war, as "the shame of Egypt, the fatal Fury of Latium, whose unchastity cost Rome dear," while Cassius Dio characterized her in his great history of Rome as "a woman of insatiable lust and greed."[4]

The Roman view of Cleopatra was summed up for the next millennium and beyond by the fourth century C.E. author of a capsule biography of the queen:

> Cleopatra, daughter of Ptolemy, king of the Egyptians, defeated by Ptolemy, her brother and husband, whom she wished to cheat of the kingdom, came to Caesar in Alexandria in the midst of civil war. She obtained Ptolemy's kingdom and his death from Caesar through her beauty and sex. She was so lustful that she often prostituted herself, so beautiful that many men purchased a night with her at the cost of their life. Later, she married Antony and suffered defeat with him. After she falsely informed him that she had committed suicide, she died in her tomb from the bite of snakes.[5]

The hostile Roman image of Cleopatra survived because it reinforced powerful cultural prejudices and fears. Men feared the potential threat to the traditional order posed by women who could control their lives and their sexuality and use it to usurp the roles of men. In the case of Cleopatra, these fears were heightened by Roman suspicion of ethnic and cultural miscegenation. For example, in the *Aeneid*—Rome's national epic—the poet Virgil modeled the Carthaginian queen Dido (who threatens to frustrate the founding of Rome by seducing the Trojan hero Aeneas) on Cleopatra.

Such fears were not limited to antiquity, and they reappeared in the Renaissance. They were enshrined in the Italian humanist Giovanni Boccaccio's pioneering biography of the queen and repeated by centuries of writers and artists. Baroque artists such as the Venetian painter Giovanni Tiepolo created elaborate paintings focused on Cleopatra's relationship with Antony, in which the honorable Roman was mesmerized by the Egyptian queen's regal elegance and extravagance. To eighteenth-century writers such as the English essayist Sarah Fielding, Cleopatra was an example of how unwomanly ambition, pride, and vanity destroyed everything it touched; nineteenth and twentieth century popular fiction and art reduced her to a symbol of the destructiveness of sexuality unrestrained by matrimony, a trend that reached its climax in the spectacular line of cinematic Cleopatras extending from Theda Bara to Elizabeth Taylor.

To be sure there were exceptions to the hostile image of Cleopatra, but they were rare. Chaucer, for example, idiosyncratically celebrated her fidelity to Antony in *The Legend of Good Women*, and Shakespeare drew on Plutarch's *Life of Antony* to draw a fully rounded picture of her as a woman in *Antony and Cleopatra*, while George Bernard Shaw neutralized the image by imagining Cleopatra as an inexperienced teenager in *Caesar and Cleopatra*. It is the hallmark of symbols, however, that they can be used for purposes different from those intended by their creators.

Not surprisingly, Cleopatra's long struggle for autonomy for Egypt and herself made her useful as a symbol for social and ethnic groups who saw themselves as victims of repressive establishments. That already in antiquity some Egyptians appropriated her as a symbol of resistance to Rome is suggested by the mummy of a young woman named Cleopatra, who lived in Thebes in the second century C.E. and whose mother was named Kandake after the Nubian queen who fought Rome to a standstill less than a decade after Cleopatra's death. A little over a century and a half later, Zenobia, the Arab queen of Palmyra who raised most of the Near East against Rome and even conquered Egypt, claimed descent from Cleopatra. More recently, the nineteenth century American sculptor William Wetmore Story's famous 1862 statue of Cleopatra with African features transformed the queen into an effective abolitionist symbol, and feminist historians have viewed Cleopatra as the paradigm of a woman who is a historical actor in her own right. So Grace Macurdy noted in her pioneering study of Hellenistic queens that "she was, whatever the mixture of her blood, the last royal Macedonian, and in her their glory ends in a sunset of splendor."[6] The most forthright in claiming Cleopatra for their own, however, have been African Americans.

For much of the twentieth century C.E., African American writers have claimed that Cleopatra was part Egyptian and that if she lived in the United States, she would be considered black according to the infamous "one drop" rule—that is, that even one drop of "black blood" makes a person black.[7] The theory has enjoyed widespread popularity, particularly in popular culture. Not only does viewing Cleopatra as black allow African Americans to claim as their own one of the most famous individuals in ancient history, but it also provides a platform from which to critique mainstream American culture. A good example is the blaxploitation film *Cleopatra Jones* in which a black female super-spy exposes police brutality against the Los Angeles black community.[8]

Criticism of the theory that Cleopatra was black has been fierce and for understandable reasons.[9] Evidence supporting the theory, as the critics insist, is thin, consisting only of Strabo's claim that Cleopatra was "illegitimate," the sources' silence concerning the identity of Cleopatra's grandmother and mother, and the assumption that in the first century B.C.E. all persons classified as Egyptian were black. Applying a nineteenth-century American definition of "blackness" to ancient Egyptians and Greeks, who did not classify peoples by race, is, however, anachronistic, so it is not surprising that until recently, most historians have rejected this interpretation of Cleopatra[10] and continued to view her as of "pure" Macedonian ancestry.

Yet the question underlying the African American reading of Cleopatra remains valid: "Who wrote the books?"[11] For almost two millennia, historians have been forced to rely almost entirely on sources written by her enemies to reconstruct the biography of the last of the Ptolemies. As the recent publication of a decree on a papyrus signed by Cleopatra indicates, archaeology offers the possibility that Cleopatra may again speak in her own voice. Hopefully, the discovery and exploration of the submerged remains of her palace in Alexandria harbor will fulfill that promise and finally replace Cleopatra the symbol with Cleopatra the queen.

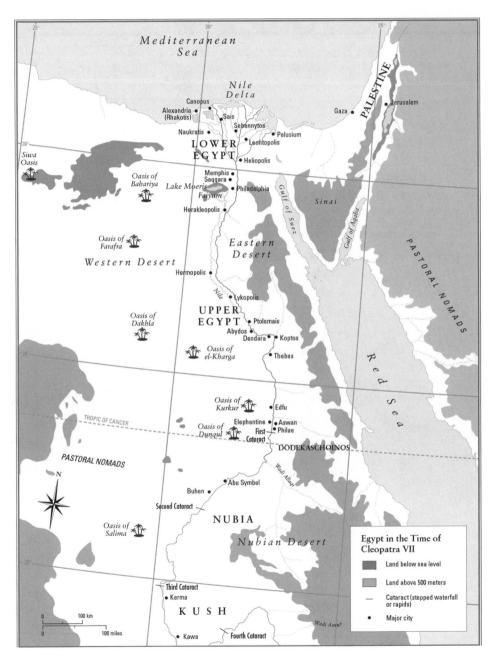

Egypt in the time of Cleopatra VII.

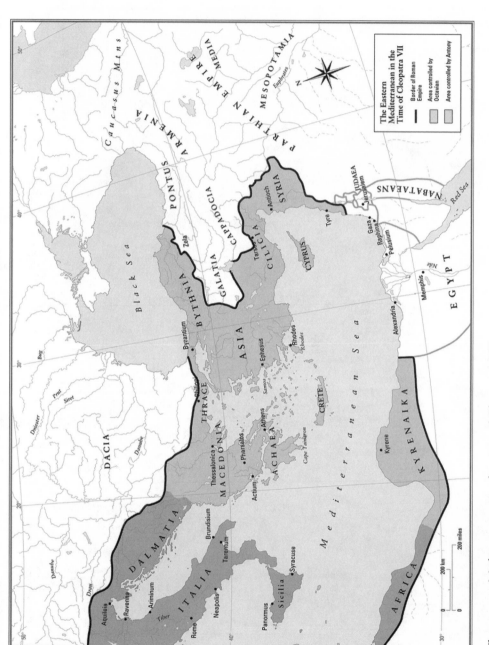

The eastern Mediterranean in the time of Cleopatra VII.

Bust of Cleopatra VII. *Antikensammlung, Staatliche Museen zu Berlin.* ©
Bildarchiv Preussischer Kulturbesitz / Art Resource, NY.

Papyrus with subscription by Cleopatra VII. Decree granting exeption to Q. Cascellius.
Aegyptisches Museum, Staatliche Museen zu Berlin. © Bildarchiv Preussischer Kulturbesitz /
Art Resource, NY.

Cleopatra's men. Bust of Julius Caesar. *Uffizi, Florence.* © *Alinari / Art Resource, NY.*

Cleopatra's men. Bust of Mark Antony. *Vatican Museums, Vatican State.* © *Alinari / Art Resource, NY.*

Cleopatra VII as her subjects saw her. Coin of Cleopatra VII. *British Museum, London.* © *Werner Forman / Art Resource, NY.*

Cleopatra VII and Caesarion worshiping Hathor. Outer wall of the Temple of Hathor at Dendera. © *Erich Lessing / Art Resource, NY.*

Reverse of coin issued to commemorate the Roman victory at Actium. Crocodile with the inscription "AEGYPT CAPTA" (Egypt Captured). *British Museum, London.* © *Werner Forman / Art Resource, NY.*

Bronze head of the Emperor Augustus found at Meroe in the Sudan. *British Museum, London.* © *Werner Forman / Art Resource, NY.*

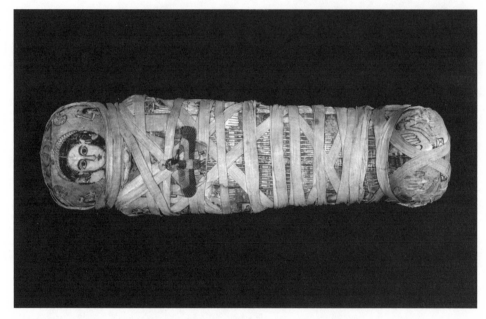

Cleopatra VII as symbol of resistance to Rome. The mummy of Cleopatra, daughter of Kandake from Thebes (second century C.E.). © *British Museum.*

Coin of the Roman Emperor Antoninus Pius (138–161 c.e.). The Goddess Isis, protector of sailors, holding a sail with the Pharos lighthouse in the background. *National Maritime Museum, Haifa.* © *Erich Lessing / Art Resource, NY.*

Statue of Cleopatra with African features. William Wetmore Story (1862). Los Angeles County Museum of Art.

BIOGRAPHIES: SIGNIFICANT FIGURES IN THE REIGN OF CLEOPATRA VII

The sixteen brief biographies in this section deal with figures who are important for understanding the life of Cleopatra VII. Because the events of Cleopatra's reign intersected both Ptolemaic and Roman history, these figures include both Greeks and Romans. Also included, moreover, are brief accounts of the ancient Egyptian goddess Isis and the Greco-Egyptian god Sarapis, which played major roles in the cultural history of Ptolemaic Egypt.

Alexander the Great (356–323 B.C.E.)

Alexander III of Macedon was born in 356 B.C.E., the first child of Philip II (382–336 B.C.E.) and his principal wife, Olympias. As heir to the throne of Macedon, he was trained by his father for his role as king. Philip assigned the philosopher Aristotle to oversee his education. He also made sure that Alexander had military experience, giving him command of the cavalry in the decisive battle of Chaeronea in 338 B.C.E. that established Macedonian authority in Greece. Alexander was, therefore, ready to assume power when Philip was assassinated in the summer of 336 B.C.E.

Alexander inherited a reformed and strengthened Macedonian army and his father's plans for the invasion of the Persian Empire. During the first two years of his reign, Alexander consolidated his power, brutally crushing a rebellion by the Greek city of Thebes and securing approval by the Greeks of the war against Persia and his position as its commander. He then crossed into Asia in the spring of 334 B.C.E. with an army of about thirty-five thousand men. During the next decade, Alexander campaigned as far as western India before a mutiny by his troops forced him to return to the west, where he died in Babylon in June 323 B.C.E.

Alexander's Persian campaign divides into three distinct phases. The first phase, which lasted from 334 B.C.E. to 330 B.C.E., included the great set battles of Granicus, Issus, and Gaugamela and ended with the destruction of the Persian capital Perepolis and the assassination of the Persian king Darius III by his own officers. The second phase lasted from 330 B.C.E. to 327 B.C.E. These three years were spent campaigning in central Asia and included some of the most difficult fighting in the whole campaign. During this period, Alexander adopted various aspects of Persian royal ceremonial practice despite strong Macedonian and Greek opposition in order to attract Iranian support in the face of fierce guerrilla resistance in central Asia. The final phase of the campaign extended from 327 B.C.E. to the summer of 323 B.C.E. and included the two years Alexander spent in India, his disastrous return to Mesopotamia through the deserts of Baluchistan, and his death at Babylon.

Alexander's involvement with Egypt was brief. It began with the surrender of Egypt by its last Persian satrap (governor) in the winter of 332/1 B.C.E. and ended with Alexander's departure for the interior of the Persian Empire in April 331 B.C.E. The highpoint of these few months was Alexander's recognition as son of Ammon by the priests of the temple of Ammon in the oasis of Siwah, an identification that radically changed his conception of himself and the nature of his kingship. Alexander also, however, established good relations with the Egyptian priesthood by sacrificing to Apis and other Egyptian gods, and founded Alexandria as a Greek city and began its construction. Alexander's conquest of Egypt, therefore, was of fundamental importance for his reign and those of the Ptolemies, who succeeded him.

Antony (Marcus Antonius) (83–30 B.C.E.)

Antony was born in 83 B.C.E. into a distinguished Roman political family. Through his mother, he was related to the family of Julius Caesar. His grandfather and father received the first of the extraordinary military commands that played a significant role in weakening the republic in the first century B.C.E.

Antony's own career began in the 50s B.C.E. He was a successful cavalry officer during the governorship of Syria of Aulus Gabinius (57–54 B.C.E.), taking part in campaigns in Palestine and Egypt. He is reported to have moderated the extent of Ptolemy XII's retaliation against his enemies after his restoration to the throne. Legend also claimed that he met and fell in love with the fifteen-year-old Cleopatra at the time of her father's return, but that is unlikely. Antony's career rapidly improved after he joined the army of Julius Caesar in Gaul. Except for a year (53/2 B.C.E.) during which he defended Caesar's interests in Rome as tribune, Antony remained in Gaul until 50 B.C.E.

Antony's relations with Caesar grew closer in the 40s B.C.E. In 47 B.C.E. he held the office of Master of the Horse, Caesar's chief deputy during his first dictatorship; and three years later he was Caesar's colleague in the consulship. After Caesar's death, he assumed the leadership of the Caesarian faction and arranged a truce between the Caesarians and the Senate. He initially underestimated the threat posed by Octavian and was almost eliminated by him and his senatorial allies in 43 B.C.E. The support of Lepidus, the governor of Gaul, however, enabled him to survive. Together with Octavian and Lepidus he formed the Second Triumvirate. He and his allies eliminated their enemies at Rome and built up their financial resources by conducting a wide-ranging proscription. A year later Antony's military skill and leadership was instrumental in defeating the senatorial forces led by Brutus and Cassius in the Battle of Philippi.

Antony was at the peak of his prestige and power immediately after the Battle of Philippi. As a result, he took Gaul and the rich provinces of the eastern Mediterranean as his share of the empire, and he spent much of 41 B.C.E. reorganizing the entire territory from Greece to Egypt, confirming or replacing rulers and collecting indemnities from those who had supported Brutus and Cassius. A year later, the outbreak of war in Italy led by his wife and brother led him to the brink of hostilities with Octavian. War was avoided and peace was confirmed by his marriage to Octavian's sister Octavia, by whom he had two daughters, Antonia Major and Antonia Minor. Throughout the 30s B.C.E., Antony's position relative to Octavian's steadily declined. War finally broke out in 32 B.C.E., ending with the defeat of Antony and Cleopatra's naval forces at Actium in 31 B.C.E. and their suicides a year later. Ironically, Antony's bloodline outlasted that of Octavian since his descendants included the emperors Caligula, Claudius, and Nero.

Arsinoe II (316–c. 270 B.C.E.)

Arsinoe was the eldest child of Ptolemy I and his second wife, Berenike. She was born on the Aegean island of Kos in 316 B.C.E. Like other Macedonian princesses, Arsinoe was a valuable asset in the political struggles of her father. In c. 300 B.C.E., Ptolemy arranged her marriage to the sixty-year-old Lysimachos, ruler of Thrace, in order to seal an alliance directed against Ptolemy's enemies Seleukos I and Demetrios, the son of Antigonos Monophthalmos (the one-eyed), who had almost reunited Alexander's empire.

Lysimachos was polygamous, and at first the young Arsinoe was only one of his several known wives. The Egyptian alliance, however, strengthened her position at court, and Arsinoe's prominence and influence grew rapidly during the 290s and 280s B.C.E. By the late 280s B.C.E., she had become Lysimachos' principal wife, and the old king had chosen one of her sons—probably the eldest, Lysimachos—to be his heir.

Evidence of her influence is provided by her financing the construction of the Arsinoeion on Samothrace and Lysimachos' gift to her of the Black Sea city Heraklea Pontika after he suppressed the city's tyrants on the pretext they murdered their mother and his former wife, Amastris. Herakleote tradition blamed Arsinoe for Lysimachos' seizure of their city, and claimed that her governor ruled it harshly. Historians also blamed her for instigating the struggle over the succession that roiled Lysimachos' court in the late 280s B.C.E. and finally led to his death, alleging that she brought about the death of his eldest Agathokles by falsely telling his father that he had tried to seduce her.

Lysimachos' death at the battle of Korupedion in 281 B.C.E. undermined the position of Arsinoe and her sons. At first she tried to secure her position by marrying her half brother Ptolemy Keraunos (thunderbolt), who had seized the throne of Macedon. The marriage, however, was a failure. After Ptolemy Keraunos murdered two of her sons, Arsinoe fled with her surviving son, Ptolemy, first to the north Aegean island of Samothrace and then to Egypt.

Arsinoe's arrival in Egypt coincided with the outbreak of political turmoil at the court of her full brother Ptolemy II. Although the details are lost, the struggles ended only in the late 270s B.C.E., when Ptolemy II divorced and exiled his present wife—Lysimachos' daughter and Arsinoe's stepdaughter Arsinoe I—and married his sister. Ptolemy II's motives for marrying Arsinoe are unknown, but his decision was successful as Arsinoe proved to be a popular and influential queen. She and her brother became the center of a new royal cult, being deified as the Theoi Philadelphoi (the sibling loving gods), and she was the first queen to receive cult in Egyptian temples. By the time of her death c. 270 B.C.E., her influence at court, particularly on Ptolemaic policy in Greece, was recognized throughout the Greek world. Later queens—including Cleopatra VII, who modeled her Egyptian crowns on those worn by her—revered Arsinoe II as the prototype of the active queen.

Berenike IV (early 70s–55 B.C.E.) and Arsinoe IV (60s–40 B.C.E.)

The women of the last Ptolemies were as formidable as the men, so it is not surprising that Cleopatra's most important rivals were her sisters, Berenike IV and Arsinoe IV.

Berenike IV was Cleopatra's elder sister and the only child of Ptolemy XII and his sister-wife Cleopatra V Tryphaina, born most likely in the early 70s B.C.E. Nothing is known of the early years of her life until she suddenly emerged as a rival to her father in 58 B.C.E. In that year the Alexandrian Greeks, furious at Ptolemy XII's acquiescence in the Roman annexation of Cyprus and the suicide of its king, proclaimed her and her mother joint rulers while Ptolemy XII was absent in Rome.

The joint rule of Berenike IV and her mother lasted only until sometime in 57 B.C.E., when her mother disappears from the sources, presumably having died. With Ptolemy XII likely to return and the Romans' attitude toward their coup uncertain, the Alexandrians sought a husband for Berenike. Their first choices were sons of the last Seleukid kings, but one died and the second was vetoed by Aulus Gabinius, the governor of Syria, since the union of Egypt and Syria would not be in Roman interests. A third individual, who claimed to be an illegitimate relation of the Seleukids, lasted less than a week as Berenike's husband before his vulgarity so disgusted her that she had him murdered. More successful was her marriage to Archelaos, who claimed to be a son of Rome's great enemy Mithridates VI of Pontus but was more likely related to his general Archelaos.

Berenike IV's brief reign ended tragically in 55 B.C.E., when Gabinius invaded Egypt and restored Ptolemy XII to power. Archelaos died defending Egypt against the Roman invaders, and Berenike IV was executed shortly after by her father. Seven years after the death of Berenike IV, Cleopatra faced an equally dangerous rival in her younger sister, Arsinoe IV.

Arsinoe IV first appears in the sources in the summer of 48 B.C.E. As part of his settlement of the dispute between Cleopatra and her brother Ptolemy XIII, Caesar assigned Cyprus to Arsinoe IV and her younger brother, the future Ptolemy XIV. Frustrated by Caesar's failure to actually transfer Cyprus to her control, Arsinoe IV—with her tutor, the eunuch Ganymedes—fled to the Egyptian army that was advancing on Alexandria and was proclaimed queen. When Ganymedes arranged the assassination of the army's commander, Achillas, Arsinoe IV became the heart of the resistance to Caesar.

Caesar failed to split the resistance by releasing Ptolemy XIII, as the young king joined forces with his sister. Their joint reign quickly ended with Ptolemy XIII's death in the Battle of the Nile and Arsinoe IV's capture by Caesar's forces. Although Arsinoe IV appeared in Caesar's triumph in 46 B.C.E., the sympathy of the Roman populace persuaded Caesar to send her into exile in the Temple of Artemis in Ephesus instead of killing her. Six years later, however, Antony ordered her execution as part of his agreement with Cleopatra, thereby removing the last threat to her power in Egypt.

Cleopatra Selene (40–c. 5 B.C.E.)

Cleopatra's death did not mean the end of her family. She had four children: Caesarion by Julius Caesar, and the twins Cleopatra Selene and Alexander Helios and their younger brother Ptolemy Philadelphos by Mark Antony. Although Octavian rebuffed her efforts to save her kingdom for her children and murdered Caesarion, he spared the twins and Ptolemy Philadelphos.

Little is known of their lives before they came into Octavian's power. Cleopatra Selene and Alexander Helios first appear in 37 B.C.E., when Antony recognized them as his own at Antioch. Cleopatra also probably engaged the philosopher and historian Nikolaos of Damaskos as her children's primary tutor. Three years later, they took center stage at the so-called Donations of Alexandria, the carefully staged pageant Cleopatra and Antony put on at Alexandria as part of the celebration of his conquest of Armenia. Cleopatra Selene is not mentioned in Plutarch's account of the division of territories that took place then, but other sources indicate that she received Kyrenaika and part of Crete. Coins issued with an image of a crocodile on the reverse side commemorated her authority over her new realm.

Cleopatra Selene's reign over Kyrenaika and Crete ended in 30 B.C.E. Octavian introduced her and her brothers to Rome during his triumph the next year. A relief recently discovered in the ruins of his monument at Nicopolis shows the children riding with him in his chariot during the triumph. Afterward, Octavia took charge of their rearing, while Octavian treated them as part of his extended family. The disappearance of her brothers from the historical record after the triumph suggests that unlike their sister, they died soon after their arrival in Rome.

Roman girls were considered ready for marriage in their teens, and Cleopatra Selene was no exception. At Octavia's suggestion, Octavian arranged her marriage to Juba II, the young king of the recently conquered kingdom of Mauretania in north Africa. The date of the marriage is unknown, but it probably occurred between Juba's accession in 25 B.C.E. and 19 B.C.E., when coins show Juba and her as rulers of Mauretania.

During the almost two decades of her marriage, Cleopatra Selene and Juba transformed the Mauretanian capital of Iol into a center of Greek and Roman culture named Caesaria. She also tried to maintain the legacy of her mother, issuing coins with types similar to those struck during her reign over Kyrenaika and Crete and naming her son Ptolemy. The line of Cleopatra did not end with Cleopatra Selene's death about 5 B.C.E. Two children of Cleopatra Selene and Juba are known. Her daughter, Drusilla, married a freedman of the emperor Claudius, who later became procurator of Judea and in that capacity remanded St. Paul to Rome for trial; while her son, Ptolemy, ruled Mauretania from Juba's death in 23 or 24 C.E. until his murder by the emperor Caligula sometime between

37 and 41 C.E. With them finally ended the long line of the descendants of Ptolemy I.

Cleopatra Thea (the Goddess) (c. 165–121/0 B.C.E.)

One of the most characteristic features of Cleopatra's reign was the influence on her actions of precedents provided by her ancestors. Most obvious is her interest in Ptolemy II and his wife Arsinoe II, but they were not the only ones. As her adoption of the title Thea Neotera—the Younger Goddess—indicates, also she was influenced by the example of her great aunt, Cleopatra Thea.

Not only was this remarkable woman the wife of three Seleukid kings and the mother of three others, but she even briefly ruled the Seleukid empire in her own name, the only queen to do so in that kingdom's history. Cleopatra Thea was born c. 165 B.C.E., the eldest daughter of Ptolemy VI Philometor and his sister-wife, Cleopatra II. Her extraordinary political career began in 150 B.C.E., when Ptolemy VI arranged her marriage to Alexander Balas as part of his plans to expand Ptolemaic influence in the Seleukid kingdom.

Balas proved an unsuitable tool, however. When his predecessor's son Demetrios II rebelled against him, the Seleukid kingdom fell into civil war. Ptolemy VI took advantage of the chaos to invade Syria in 148 B.C.E., ostensibly to help Balas and his daughter. Their alliance quickly collapsed and Ptolemy switched his support and his daughter to Demetrios II. Three years later, both Ptolemy and Balas were dead, and Cleopatra Thea was securely ensconced in Antioch as Demetrios II's queen.

The first phase of Cleopatra Thea's marriage to Demetrios II lasted six years, ending with his capture and imprisonment by the Parthians in 139 B.C.E. It produced three children, the future kings Seleukos V (126/5 B.C.E.) and Antiochos VIII Grypos (125–96 B.C.E.) and a daughter named Laodike. A year after Demetrios' imprisonment, Cleopatra Thea married her third husband—Demetrios II's younger brother, Antiochos VII. This marriage produced four more children including another king, Antiochos IX Kyzikenos (115–95 B.C.E.). Her third marriage ended similarly to the second, as Antiochos VII was killed in 129 B.C.E. while trying unsuccessfully to win back Babylonia and Iran from the Parthians. Even worse, Demetrios II escaped from the Parthians and returned to Syria, resuming his reign and his marriage to Cleopatra Thea after a twelve-year absence. Three years later, Demetrios II was killed in yet another civil war, and Cleopatra Thea seized the opportunity to assume power in her own name.

Cleopatra Thea's unprecedented sole reign was limited in both time and extent, lasting less than a year and being limited to Phoenicia. Her break with tradition was too great, and by 125 B.C.E. she had been forced to associate her son Antiochos VIII with her as co-regent. On their joint coinage, however, she always took precedence over him, the inscription reading "Queen Cleopatra and King Antiochos." The life of this remarkable woman, whose career in many ways recalls that of Cleopatra VII, ended tragically in 121 B.C.E., when her son poisoned her, allegedly with the poison she had intended for him.

Herod the Great (73–4 B.C.E.)

Herod was born in 73 B.C.E. to an influential family in Idumea in southern Palestine that had converted to Judaism in the second century B.C.E. His family owed its political prominence to the decision of his father, Antipater, to support Pompey when he suppressed the Jewish monarchy in 63 B.C.E. and established Roman rule in Judaea. Antipater further strengthened his family's influence in 47 B.C.E. by providing troops to Caesar, who rewarded him by making him a Roman citizen and appointing him procurator (governor) of Judea.

Herod's rise to power also began in 47 B.C.E. when Antipater appointed him governor of Galilee. Herod survived by skillfully maneuvering through the complex politics of the 40s B.C.E. During the war that followed Caesar's death, Herod supported Cassius, the senatorial governor of Syria, who appointed him governor of Koile Syria in return. After the Battle of Philippi, however, Herod adroitly switched sides and succeeded in excusing himself and establishing good relations with Antony, who persuaded the Senate to recognize him as king of the Jews in 40 B.C.E.

Herod's remarkable political dexterity continued to be his salvation in the 30s B.C.E. Despite the Senate's decision in his favor, he was forced to take refuge in Alexandria in 40 B.C.E. because the Parthians had occupied Judea and placed his Hasmonean rival Antigonos II on the throne. Herod's initial relations with Cleopatra were good. She even tried to recruit him into Egyptian service, offering him a military command against the Parthians. By 37 B.C.E., however, the Parthians had been expelled from Judea, and Antony had executed Antigonos and restored Herod to the throne instead of awarding the kingdom to Cleopatra. As a result, relations with Cleopatra deteriorated quickly.

Antony's support continued to be critical to Herod's survival as Cleopatra schemed to gain control of Judea. For almost three years, she supported the claims of his Hasmonean rivals to the high priesthood, even forcing him to defend himself before Antony against charges of murder. Even though Antony exonerated him, Herod still had to make territorial concessions to Cleopatra. Herod could only take revenge for his frustration in his memoirs, boasting that he had rejected both Cleopatra's attempt to seduce him and his advisors' advice to assassinate her during her visit to Judea in 34 B.C.E.

Ever the opportunist, Herod ensured his survival after the Battle of Actium by transferring his allegiance to Octavian, entertaining him in Judea and providing money and troops for his invasion of Egypt. Octavian rewarded Herod handsomely for his change of sides, confirming his position as king of the Jews, returning to him the territories Antony had given Cleopatra together with a number of additional cities, and even giving him Cleopatra's Gallic bodyguard. For the next twenty-six years, Herod ruled Judea as a loyal Roman client king. During those years, he carried out an extensive building program at home that included the second temple at Jerusalem, a splendid port at Caesaria, and numerous forts while acting as a patron of Hellenism throughout the eastern Mediterranean.

Isis

Isis was one of the oldest and most important of Egyptian deities. Sister and wife of Osiris and mother of Horos, she occupied a central place in the charter myth of Egyptian kingship. Ptolemaic patronage of her cult dated to the reign of Ptolemy II, who built a great temple in her honor on the island of Philae, south of the first cataract of the Nile. Because of her role as royal wife and mother, however, Ptolemaic queens especially honored her, most notably Cleopatra VII, who identified herself with Isis.

According to Egyptian tradition, Isis was part of the Ennead of Heliopolis—the family of nine gods who created Egypt and gave birth to its first kings: Atum, the sun god and creator; Shu, the god of air, and his wife Tefnut, the goddess of moisture; Geb, the god of the earth, his wife Nut, the goddess of the sky, and their children; Osiris, the god of vegetation; his wife Isis, the goddess of magic; Seth, the god of the desert and things foreign; and his wife Nephthys. The focus of the myth was the conflict of Osiris and Seth over the kingship of Egypt. According to the story, Seth killed and dismembered Osiris, but Isis found and reassembled the scattered parts, magically reanimated them, and conceived Horos, the falcon-headed sky god. Horos defeated Seth in trial by combat, became king, and buried his father, who became king of the dead. In Egyptian belief, all subsequent Egyptian kings became Horos at their coronation and Osiris at their burial. Isis, whose name and hieroglyphic symbol indicate that she was the deified royal throne, is central to the myth since it was her magic that transformed the human king into the incarnation of Horos at his coronation and made it possible for him to perform the funeral rites that enabled his dead father to become Osiris.

Isis was the longest lived of all Egyptian gods. Her cult survived well into late antiquity, ending only in 543 c.e. when the Roman emperor Justinian I ordered the great temple on the island of Philai to be closed. Not only did Isis' cult outlast all other Egyptian cults, but it spread throughout the Roman Empire. Isis changed dramatically, however, as her cult spread outside Egypt. Through syncretism, she was identified with a variety of Greek goddesses including Demeter, Aphrodite, Athena, Persephone, and Hera. As a result, Isis became a universal deity responsible for the creation of civilization, the patron of sailors, and the protector of the family. At the same time, the significance of her connection to Osiris was revalued so that the emphasis fell on her ability to vanquish death through magic instead of her traditional role in the divine foundation of the Egyptian monarchy. In the process, she became the center of a mystery cult that offered salvation to her initiates and became a potent rival to Christianity.

Julius Caesar (100–44 B.C.E.)

Gaius Julius Caesar was born in Rome in 100 B.C.E. into an ancient patrician family that claimed descent from the goddess Venus and Aeneas, the supposed Trojan founder of Rome. Despite its distinguished ancestry, his family's political fortunes had long been in decline, until they were revived by the marriage of Caesar's aunt to the influential politician and war hero Marius.

Caesar's own political career began slowly. His family's connection to Marius and his allies brought him into conflict with the dictator Sulla in the late 80s B.C.E., but he survived. During the next decade, he studied rhetoric in Asia and saw military service in the same area. In the 60s B.C.E., his career significantly improved. The key to his success was the alliance he formed with the politician and financier Marcus Licinius Crassus. Thanks to Crassus' support, he was elected to the offices of pontifex maximus (high priest) of Rome and praetor. After his praetorship, he served as governor of Further Spain.

Booty gained during his Spanish governorship enabled Caesar to pay off his debts and move to the forefront of Roman politics. Humiliated by the Senate's refusal to allow him to celebrate his triumph, he formed the First Triumvirate with Crassus and Pompey in 60 B.C.E. Elected consul for 59 B.C.E., Caesar gained a special command for himself covering Illyria, Cisalpine Gaul (northern Italy) and Transalpine Gaul (southern France) in a consulship marked by illegality. He spent the years 58 B.C.E. to 51 B.C.E. conquering the remainder of Gaul. He also conducted raids across the Rhine River into Germany and into southern Britain, thereby establishing precedents for later Roman military activity in both areas.

Caesar's successes in Gaul threatened his partners in the First Triumvirate. When Crassus was killed in 54 B.C.E. while invading Parthia, Pompey sought security by allying with Caesar's enemies in the Senate. Relations between Caesar and Pompey steadily worsened until the civil war broke out in 49 B.C.E. Caesar quickly overran Italy, but Pompey succeeded in escaping to Greece, where Caesar defeated him at the Battle of Pharsalus in 48 B.C.E. Caesar had no serious rivals after Pompey's death in Egypt in the summer of 48 B.C.E. War in Egypt and campaigns in Anatolia, North Africa, and Spain against Pompey's surviving supporters, however, delayed his return to Rome until 46 B.C.E. Less than two years later he was dead, assassinated by a senatorial conspiracy on March 15, 44 B.C.E.

Caesar's ultimate plans for Rome and its empire and for Cleopatra's role in it have mystified historians since antiquity. What is clear is that he became steadily more autocratic after Pompey's death, holding both the consulship—Rome's highest office—every year and the dictatorship—an extraordinary office that gave its holder virtually royal power—

first for ten years and then, just before his death, for life. These actions suggested to his assassins that he wished to be king, and his close relationship to Cleopatra reinforced that belief.

Octavia (69–11 B.C.E.)

Octavia was the daughter of Gaius Octavius and Atia and the sister of Octavian. Born in 69 B.C.E., she was six years older than her brother. The sources assign her the role of the good wife in a morality play in which she and Cleopatra struggle for control of Antony's soul. In that drama, Octavia is portrayed as the good and beautiful wife, who offered Antony his last chance to save himself for Rome.

The reality was different. Like other Roman aristocratic women, Octavia's marriages were tools in the political plans of her male relatives—that is, her father and, later, her great uncle Julius Caesar and, of course, her brother. The pattern was already set in the 50s B.C.E. In 54 B.C.E. her father sought to advance his family's social and political position by arranging her marriage to Gaius Claudius Marcellus, a member of an old and distinguished patrician family, by whom she had a son, Marcus Claudius Marcellus, and two daughters named Marcella. A year later, however, Julius Caesar suggested that she divorce Marcellus in order to replace his daughter, Julia, who had just died, as Pompey's wife. Pompey refused, but Marcellus understandably became one of Caesar's bitterest enemies.

Octavia's marriage protected Marcellus until his death in 40 B.C.E. despite his hostility to Caesar. Instead of liberating her, widowhood merely made Octavia available for use in Octavian's schemes. That same year, she married Antony to seal the reconciliation between him and her brother. Antony commemorated the marriage by having a coin issued with both their portraits on it, while the poet Virgil prophesied in his fourth *Eclogue* that their expected son would herald the birth of a new Golden Age.

Octavia's marriage to Antony lasted for almost eight years and produced two daughters: Antonia Maior (the elder) and Antonia Minor (the younger). At first, the marriage seemed promising. Octavia and Antony spent the winter of 39/8 B.C.E. in Athens, where Octavia became a patron of the city's philosophers and won the hearts of the Athenians, who identified her with Athena in a sacred marriage celebrated by Antony. Her influence with Antony was still strong in 37 B.C.E. when he sent her to Italy to reaffirm the alliance with Octavian. It was, however, to be the last time she saw her husband. A year later, when she tried to bring him reinforcements, he ordered her and their children to return to Italy.

Ironically, the collapse of her marriage gave Octavia the freedom she had hitherto lacked. After returning to Rome, she lived in Antony's house in Rome and defended him against Octavian's slanders until 32 B.C.E., when he formally divorced her and married Cleopatra. After Antony's death, she again became her brother's tool, raising Antony's children and watching her daughters being married to advance Augustus' plans. After the death in 23 B.C.E. of her beloved son Marcellus, who was being groomed to be Augustus' heir, Octavia went into a seclusion that only ended with her death in 11 B.C.E.

Octavian (63 B.C.E.–14 C.E.)

Octavian was born Gaius Octavius in 63 B.C.E. to a prominent family in the Italian city of Velitrae, south of Rome. His father was the first member of his family to become a Roman Senator and hold high office at Rome, having attained the praetorship—the second ranking office in the Roman state. His mother came from a similar background and was the daughter of the sister of Julius Caesar. Octavian was, therefore, Caesar's grandnephew and closest surviving male relative.

Caesar promoted Octavian's career in the early 40s B.C.E., taking him to Spain in 45 B.C.E. for the last military campaign of the civil war and adopting him as his son and heir in late 45 B.C.E. Octavian's position changed dramatically, however, after Caesar's assassination in March 44 B.C.E. When Antony rebuffed his claim to Caesar's estate, Octavian found support among Caesar's veterans, and by 43 B.C.E., his political position was strong enough for him to be included with Antony and Marcus Lepidus in the Second Triumvirate.

During the next three years, Octavian emerged as one of the principal figures in Roman politics. Although he played a secondary role in the defeat of Brutus and Cassius and the Republican cause at the Battle of Philippi in 42 B.C.E., he quickly eclipsed Lepidus, becoming by 40 B.C.E. the dominant member of the Second Triumvirate in the west. Antony's marriage to his sister Octavia confirmed the new distribution of power.

Octavian's influence at Rome steadily increased during the first half of the 30s B.C.E. while Antony's declined. By mid-decade, he had eliminated his chief rivals in the west, Sextus Pompey and Marcus Lepidus, and was ready to challenge Antony directly. Octavian adroitly used the collapse of Antony's marriage to Octavia and Roman hostility to Cleopatra to set the stage for the war that ended in his victory in the Battle of Actium in 31 B.C.E. and the conquest of Egypt the following year.

Antony's and Cleopatra's deaths left Octavian as master of the Roman Empire. Three years later, in early 27 B.C.E., he redefined his position in the Roman state, formally ending the Second Triumvirate and officially restoring civil authority to the Senate while retaining a commanding position within the state under his new name, Augustus. During the remainder of his reign, he almost doubled the size of the empire and strengthened his control of the state, thanks to his control of the Roman Army and a complex set of powers granted him by the Senate that allowed him to influence virtually all political and administrative functions.

Egypt played a special role in Octavian's new system. Although his attempt to conquer the kingdom of Kush failed in the 20s B.C.E., his control of Egypt remained secure. Egypt was governed by an appointed prefect, and Senators could visit it only with his permission. Egypt's tribute and grain surplus remained under his control, giving him both a source of discretionary funds and control of Rome's grain supply.

Plutarch (c. 40s–c. 120s C.E.)

The dearth of primary sources for the reign of Cleopatra means that historians have to rely on secondary sources for their information. The variety of the available sources is wide and includes Appian—the second-century C.E. historian of Rome's wars—and Cassius Dio—the third-century C.E. Roman historian. The most important source, however, is the philosopher and moralist Plutarch. Not only is he the most informative source of information about Cleopatra, but his interpretation of the Egyptian queen has profoundly influenced all accounts of her reign since the Renaissance.

Plutarch was born in central Greece in the Boeotian city of Chaeronea in the 40s C.E. and died in the 120s C.E. Plutarch was the most prominent Platonic philosopher and moralist of his time, and a prolific author with over two hundred known works. Although he devoted most of his life to service to his home city and to the oracle of Apollo at Delphi, Plutarch had numerous influential Roman friends and received many high honors, including the privileges of a consul and the rank of procurator (governor) of Greece. His works were wide-ranging and varied in subject, including essays on moral and antiquarian subjects and biographical studies.

The most important of his works was *Parallel Lives*. In its present form, it consists of a series of forty-four paired lives of major Greek and Roman historical figures extending from the legendary founders of Athens and Rome to the reign of the emperor Augustus. Plutarch's purpose in writing *Parallel Lives* was to provide exemplary models of moral lives and to prove to his Greek contempories that Rome had produced heroic figures comparable to the greatest figures in Greek history.

Although Plutarch refers to Cleopatra in the lives of Pompey, Julius Caesar, and Mark Antony, it is *Life of Antony* that provides the bulk of our information concerning her. *Life of Antony* is unique for its length— it is the longest of the lives—and for its focus. Unlike the other *Parallel Lives*, the pair of Antony and Demetrios the Besieger were intended to provide examples of men of great talent who were ruined by their own personal flaws. So in Plutarch's analysis, Antony was a man of great political and military ability and courage. Those virtues, however, were vitiated by his weakness for luxury and self-indulgence in sex and drink, which Cleopatra exploited for her own purposes.

The richness of Plutarch's sources for *Life of Antony*—which included histories of Rome, the memoirs of the emperor Augustus and Cleopatra's doctor, and family traditions—enabled him to trace the relationship between Antony and Cleopatra in great detail, from their first serious encounter in 41 B.C.E. to their death a decade later. At the same time, his emphasis on the mixture of virtue and vice in Antony prevented him from providing merely a one-sided portrayal of Cleopatra as an unprincipled seductress. As a result, Plutarch provided later historians with an account of the Egyptian queen that was unique for its detail and complexity and is the basis for all modern biographies of her.

Ptolemy I Soter (the Savior) (367/366–282 B.C.E.)

Ptolemy I was born in Macedon in 367/366 B.C.E. He was the son of a noble named Lagos and a member of a family distantly related to the

Macedonian royal house. He was raised at the capital, Pella, and was one of Alexander the Great's oldest friends, even suffering exile for supporting the prince's opposition to his father's plans.

Ptolemy took part in Alexander's Persian campaign from its beginning in 334 B.C.E. to its end in 323 B.C.E. On the basis of his experiences, Ptolemy wrote a history of Alexander's reign that was favorable to the king and, although lost, is the source of much of our knowledge of the king. In 330 B.C.E., Alexander appointed him as a bodyguard—one of the eight elite cavalry officers who protected the king in battle and were his closest advisors. During the final years of the campaign, Ptolemy was assigned several independent commands and was wounded at least once in India.

Ptolemy played a prominent role in the struggle over the succession to Alexander that broke out in the summer of 323 B.C.E., taking Egypt as his satrapy. Unlike the other bodyguards, however, Ptolemy opposed the continuation of the empire as a unified state. From 323 B.C.E. onward, he pursued an essentially defensive policy, intended to secure his control of Egypt. To that end, he assassinated Kleomenes of Naukratis, Alexander's unpopular satrap of Egypt, and stole Alexander's body, bringing it to Memphis for burial. This defiance of the Macedonian regent Perdikkas provoked an unsuccessful invasion of Egypt in which Perdikkas died.

After Perdikkas' death, Ptolemy resumed his defensive policy. He refused an offer of the regency. While he joined the various alliances formed in opposition to Antigonos Monophthalmos' attempt to maintain the unity of the empire and even declared himself king in 305 B.C.E., Ptolemy avoided direct involvement in most of the resulting conflicts including the decisive Battle of Ipsos in 301 B.C.E., where Antigonos died and, with him, the last hope of reuniting Alexander's empire. Instead, Ptolemy annexed the neighboring territories of Libya, Koile Syria, and Cyprus, and extended Egyptian influence in the Aegean.

Little is known of the final years of Ptolemy's reign. His seizure of Koile Syria in 301 B.C.E. soured relations between him and Seleukos I, and led to the alliance with Lysimachos that sent his daughter Arsinoe to Thrace as Lysimachos' queen. As in the first half of his reign, however, Ptolemy avoided military action far from Egypt, focusing his efforts instead on developing his kingdom. He laid the foundations of the Ptolemaic administrative system and built extensively at Alexandria, beginning the construction of the Pharos lighthouse and founding the Museum and Library. He also encouraged Greek immigration and began the large-scale settlement of Jews in Egypt by settling prisoners captured in the conquest of Jerusalem in 307 B.C.E. He also ordered the creation of the god Sarapis. Ptolemy finally died in 282 B.C.E., having first ensured the succession to his throne by making Ptolemy II—his son by his second wife, Berenike—his co-ruler.

Ptolemy II Philadelphos (Sibling Lover) (308–246 B.C.E.)

Ptolemy II was born on the Aegean island of Cos in 308 B.C.E., the younger child of Ptolemy I and his second wife, Berenike. Nothing is known of his early life until 285 B.C.E., when his father exiled his first wife, Eurydike, and their son, Ptolemy Keraunos, and made Ptolemy II his co-regent. Three years later, he became king on the death of Ptolemy I.

Ptolemy II's long reign was dominated by foreign affairs. Although relations between Ptolemy I and Seleukos I had become tense following the Egyptian king's occupation of Koile Syria in 301 B.C.E., the outbreak of hostilities was delayed until the accession of Ptolemy II, who fought three wars with the Seleukid rulers Antiochos I and Antiochos II. Hostilities did not remain confined to Ptolemaic and Seleukid forces but spilled over into Greece, where Ptolemy II supported Athens and Sparta in the Chremonidean War (267–262 B.C.E.), and Nubia, where he organized large-scale elephant hunts in order to counter his Seleukid opponents' monopoly of Indian elephants. While Ptolemy II lost several major naval battles, he ultimately emerged victorious in his wars with the Seleukids. Not only did he preserve the territories he inherited from his father, but he expanded Ptolemaic holdings in the Aegean and northern Nubia and gained significant influence in Syria as a result of the marriage of his daughter Berenike to Antiochos II in the late 250s B.C.E. By the time of his death in 246 B.C.E., Egyptian influence extended throughout the eastern Mediterranean and reached westward to Sicily, Carthage, and even Rome.

Ptolemy II's reign was also of fundamental importance for the internal development of Ptolemaic Egypt. To finance his expansive foreign policy, he reorganized and systematized the Egyptian administrative system, transforming key areas of the economy into government monopolies, increasing taxes, and extending governmental supervision over the Egyptian temples and their revenues. He also strengthened the position of the royal family, establishing the tradition of royal incest by marrying his sister Arsinoe II. He also created a focus of loyalty for his subjects in the dynastic cult by deifying his parents as the Theoi Soteres (savior gods). Finally, he became the first Ptolemy to be deified in his lifetime by associating himself with Arsinoe II after her death in the cult of the Theoi Philadelphoi (sibling loving gods).

Ptolemy II was also famous in antiquity as a patron of culture. He completed construction of the Pharos lighthouse and cultural centers including the Museum and Library as well as numerous Greek and Egyptian temples. He is reported to have sponsored the Greek translation of the Jewish Bible known as the *Septuagint*, and was the patron of numerous writers and intellectuals, including the poets Kallimakhos and Theokritos, the Egyptian historian Manetho, and the doctors Herophilos and Erasistratos. Ptolemy II's combination of an active foreign policy with far-reaching state oversight of the economy and culture inspired many later Ptolemaic rulers, including Cleopatra VII, who named her last son after him and sought to re-create his empire.

Ptolemy XII Neos Dionysos (the Young Dionysos) (late 2nd century–51 B.C.E.)

Ptolemy XII was the son of Ptolemy IX Soter II and an unknown woman. The date of his birth is also unknown, but it probably fell within the last two decades of the second century B.C.E. Ptolemy XII's youth coincided with the bitter struggle for the throne of Egypt between the two sons of Ptolemy VIII—his father, Ptolemy IX Soter II, and his uncle, Ptolemy X Alexander I. As a result, Ptolemy XII was forced to spend much of his early life in exile.

Ptolemy XII's exile began in 103 B.C.E. when Cleopatra III sent him and his bother to the Aegean island of Kos for protection. The brothers' exile lasted for over two decades. Not all of it, however, was spent on Kos. In 86 B.C.E., they became pawns in the struggle for dominance of the eastern Mediterranean between Rome and Mithridates VI of Pontus, when Mithridates occupied Kos, kidnapped the brothers, and engaged them to two of his daughters as part of a plan to extend his influence to Egypt.

The brothers' fortunes changed for the better in 80 B.C.E. Infuriated by his murder of the popular Cleopatra Berenike III, the Alexandrian Greeks assassinated Ptolemy XI Alexander III and summoned the brothers back from exile, making Ptolemy XII king of Egypt and his brother king of Cyprus. To consolidate his hold on power, Ptolemy XII followed tradition and married his sister Cleopatra Tryphaina by whom he had a daughter, Cleopatra Berenike IV. Later in the decade he formed a relationship, which Greeks considered illegitimate, with another woman, possibly Egyptian, by whom he had four children: Cleopatra VII, Arsinoe IV, Ptolemy XIII, and Ptolemy XIV.

The evidence for Ptolemy XII's long reign is limited but clearly indicates that it was turbulent. For example, his wife Cleopatra V disappeared in 69 B.C.E. for a decade before reemerging briefly in the early 50s B.C.E. as co-regent with her daughter, in a coup directed against her former husband. It was the threat from Rome, however, that dominated his reign. Historians have given him little credit for the skill with which he survived and maintained the independence of Egypt for three decades by exploiting the suspicions of Roman politicians, who feared that allowing anyone to gain credit for annexing Egypt would destabilize the political balance of power at Rome. At the same time, he successfully rebuilt support for dynasty among the powerful Egyptian priesthood through an extensive program of temple construction, and transformed the nature of the royal cult by being the first Ptolemy to identify himself during his lifetime with a particular Greek god, Dionysos. By so doing, he laid a strong foundation for the reign of his daughter Cleopatra VII.

Sarapis

From the beginning of their history, Greeks had encountered the gods of other peoples. They had solved the problem of whether or not these gods were the same as their own through the process of identification historians call syncretism. Sarapis was the most remarkable result of this process.

Sarapis was the patron god of the Ptolemaic dynasty and the city god of Alexandria. Sarapis and his cult were deliberate creations intended to provide a link between Greeks, Macedonians, and Egyptians. Although there is evidence that Sarapis was already being worshiped in the late fourth century B.C.E., the decisive period for the development of the god was the third century B.C.E.

In his final form, Sarapis included aspects drawn from many gods, both Greek and Egyptian, including Pluto, ruler of the underworld; the Egyptian god Osiris; Zeus: the healing god Asklepios; Dionysos; and the sun god Helios. His origin was the Memphite god Osarapis (Wsir-Hapi), who was already worshiped by Greeks in the late fourth century B.C.E. Osarapis was the deified soul of the Apis bull when it manifested itself as Osiris, king of the dead. At the Serapeum, his home in Memphis and the burial place of the Apis bulls, Osarapis provided cures and oracles through dreams to his devotees.

The cult of Sarapis at Memphis remained close to its roots in the cults of Osiris and Apis. The situation was different at Alexandria. Although Ptolemy I built the city's principal temple of Sarapis in the Egyptian quarter of Rhakotis, Greek influence on the cult was strong. The Ptolemaic government played a major role in the development of Sarapis. The most important contributions were made by the Athenian priest Timotheos of Eleusis and the Egyptian historian Manetho. They identified Sarapis and Pluto, an identification that was facilitated by the fact that both Pluto and Osiris were kings of the dead. Identifications with other gods quickly followed, transforming Sarapis into a universal deity. Ptolemy I also had the sculptor Bryaxis create a regal cult statue appropriate to this new vision of Sarapis, and encouraged the story that Sarapis had revealed to him in a dream the location of his new statue.

The cult was further elaborated by Ptolemy I's successors. Ptolemy II added a library to the god's temple, while Ptolemy III replaced Sarapis' existing temple with a new and larger temple that lasted until the fourth century C.E. and linked it to a new temple of Isis. Finally, Ptolemy IV added to the complex a temple of Harpokrates—the Greek form of the Egypt sky-god Horos, the divine counterpart of the king. The result was that Sarapis became the central figure in a Hellenized version of the ancient Egyptian royal cult of Osiris, Isis, and Horos; and in Egypt, dedications to Sarapis were commonly made on behalf of the king and his family. His cult also spread widely outside Egypt, but there the focus shifted to emphasize his role as a healing and oracular god, who offered the hope of salvation after death.

PRIMARY DOCUMENTS CONCERNING CLEOPATRA VII

DOCUMENT 1
The Reign of Cleopatra

Historians are fortunate to have Julius Caesar's autobiographical account of the conflict that led to Cleopatra's rise to power. Civil War *tells the story of the conflict between Caesar and the forces of the Senate and Pompey from the outbreak of fighting in 50 B.C.E. to the beginning of the siege of Alexandria two years later. The story of the siege itself is told in* Alexandrian War, *a continuation of* Civil War *written by one of Caesar's officers. Neither work, however, tells how Cleopatra and Caesar met. Fortunately, that omission is remedied by Plutarch. Unfortunately, for the remainder of Cleopatra's reign, historians have to rely on the account provided by Plutarch in his* Life of Antony. *Although he wrote almost two centuries after Cleopatra's death, Plutarch used a variety of contemporary sources, including the accounts of some of Cleopatra's palace staff, in order to draw a vivid picture of the queen during the last years of her life.*

Pompey tries to escape to Egypt after the Battle of Pharsalus, but is murdered by the supporters of Ptolemy XIII.

There [at Pelusium] by chance was King Ptolemy, a boy in years, waging war with large forces against his sister Kleopatra, whom a few months before he had expelled from the throne by the help of his relations and friends. The camp of Kleopatra was not far distant from his camp. To him

Pompey sent begging to be received in Alexandria and supported in his calamity by the king's resources, in remembrance of the hospitality and friendship that he had shown his father. But his messengers, having fulfilled the duty of their embassy, began to converse more freely with the king's soldiers and to exhort them to show their dutiful loyalty to Pompey, and not to despise his fortunes. In the number of these men were very many soldiers of Pompey, whom Gabinius had taken over from his army in Syria and had transported to Alexandria, and on the conclusion of the war had left them with Ptolemy, the youth's father.

Then, on learning of these proceedings, the king's friends, who, on account of his youth, were in charge of the kingdom, whether moved by fear, as they afterwards gave out, lest Pompey should seize on Alexandria and Egypt after tampering with the royal army, or because they despised his fortunes, according to the common rule that in misfortune friends become enemies. They gave in public a generous reply to his messengers and bade him visit the king, but themselves formed a secret plot, and sent Achillas, the king's prefect, a man of singular audacity, and L. Septimius, a military tribune, to assassinate Pompey. And he, being courteously addressed by them and being lured forth by some previous knowledge of Septimius, because he had been a centurion under him in the pirate war, embarked in a little boat with a few of his friends, and is thereupon assassinated by Achillas and Septimius. L. Lentulus is also arrested by the king and slain in prison.

Julius Caesar arrives in Egypt shortly after the death of Pompey and asserts his authority over the country.

At Alexandria he learns of the death of Pompey, and there immediately on landing he hears the shouting of the soldiers whom the king had left in the town on garrison duty and sees them hurrying to meet him, because the fasces were being carried in front of him. Hereby the whole multitude asserted that the royal authority was being infringed. When this tumult was appeased frequent disturbances took place on successive days from the gathering of the multitude, and many soldiers were killed in all parts of this town.

Observing these events, he ordered other legions, which he had made up out of the Pompeian troops to be brought him from Asia. For he was himself compulsorily detained by the etesian winds, which blow directly counter to those sailing from Alexandria. Meanwhile, thinking that the controversies of the princes affected the Roman people and himself as consul, and concerned his functions all the more because in his previous consulship an alliance had been formed with the elder Ptolemy both by legislative enactment and by decree of the senate, he declares that it is his pleasure that King Ptolemy and his sister Kleopatra should disband the armies that they controlled, and should settle their disputes by process of law before himself rather than by armed force between themselves.

On account of the king's youth his tutor, a eunuch named Pothinus, was in charge of the kingdom. He at first began to complain among his friends and express his indignation that the king should be summoned to plead his cause; then, finding certain persons among the king's friends to abet his plot, he secretly summoned the army from Pelusium to Alexandria and put the same Achillas, whom we have mentioned above, in command of all the forces. This man, puffed up as he was by his own and the king's promises, he urged to action, and informed him by letter and messenger what he wished to be done. In the will of their father Ptolemy the elder of the two sons and the elder of the two daughters were inscribed as heirs. In the same will Ptolemy adjured the Roman people in the name of all the gods and of the treaties which he had made at Rome to carry out these provisions. One copy of the will had been taken to Rome by his envoys to be placed in the treasury, but had been deposited with Pompey because it had not been possible to place it there owing to the embarrassments of the state; a second duplicate copy was left sealed for production at Alexandria.

When these matters were being dealt with by Caesar, and he was particularly desirous of settling the disputes of the princes as a common friend and arbitrator, word is suddenly brought that the royal army and all the cavalry are on their way to Alexandria. Caesar's forces were by no means so large that he could trust them if he had to fight outside the town. It remained that he should keep in his own position in the town and learn the intentions of Achillas. But he ordered all his men to stand by their arms, and exhorted the king to send to Achillas those of his friends whom he judged to be of chief authority and to explain what his intentions were. Accordingly Dioscorides and Serapion, who had both been envoys at Rome and had possessed great influence with his father Ptolemy, were commissioned by the king and came to Achillas. And when they had come into his presence, before hearing them or learning for what reason they had been sent he ordered them to be arrested and killed. And one of them, having received a wound, was promptly snatched away by his friends and carried off for dead; the other was slain. After this deed Caesar manages to bring the king under his own control, because he thinks that the king's title had great weight with his subjects, and in order to make it apparent that the war had been undertaken on the private initiative of a small clique and a set of brigands rather than on that of the king.

The forces with Achillas were not such as to seem contemptible in respect of number or grade of men or experience in warfare. For he had twenty thousand men under arms. These consisted of soldiers of Gabinius who had habituated themselves to Alexandrian life and license and had unlearnt the name and discipline of the Roman people and married wives by whom very many of them had children. To them were added men collected from among the freebooters and brigands of Syria and the province of Cilicia and the neighboring regions; also many condemned criminals and exiles had joined them. All our own fugitive slaves had a sure place of refuge at Alexandria, and assurance of their lives on the condition of giving in their names and being on the army roll; and if any one of them was arrested by his owner he would be rescued by the common consent of the soldiery, who repelled violence done to their comrades as a peril to their own selves, since they were all alike involved in similar guilt. These men had been in the habit of demanding for execution the friends of the princes, of plundering the property of the rich, of besetting the king's palace to secure an increase of pay, of driving one man from the throne and summoning another to fill it, after an ancient custom of the Alexandrian army. There were besides two thousand cavalry. All these had grown old in the numerous wars at Alexandria, had restored the elder Ptolemy to the throne, had killed the two sons of Bibulus, and had waged war with the Egyptians. Such was their experience in warfare.

Ptolemaic forces led by Achillas attempt to break into the palace but are defeated by Caesar, who burns the Egyptian fleet and seizes control of Pharos.

On the island there is a tower called Pharos, of great height, a work of wonderful construction, which took its name from the island. This island, lying over against Alexandria, makes a harbor, but it is connected with the town by a narrow roadway like a bridge, piers nine hundred feet in length having been thrown out seawards by former kings. On this island there are dwelling-houses of Egyptians and a settlement the size of a town, and any ships that went a little out of their course there through carelessness or rough weather they were in the habit of plundering like pirates. Moreover, on account of the narrowness of the passage there can be no entry for ships into the harbor without the consent of those who are in occupation of Pharos. Caesar, now fearing such difficulty, landed his troops when the enemy was occupied in fighting, and seized Pharos and placed a garrison on it. The result of these measures was that corn and reinforcements could be safely conveyed to him on shipboard. For he sent messengers to all the neighboring provinces and summoned reinforcements from them. In the remaining parts of the town the result of the fighting was that they separated after an indecisive engagement and neither side was beaten, the reason of this being the narrowness of the space; and a few men having been slain on both sides, Caesar drew a cordon round the most necessary positions and strengthened the defenses by night. In this region of the town there was a small part of the palace to which he had been at first conducted for his personal residence, and a theatre was attached to the house, which took the place of a citadel, and had approaches to the port and to the other docks. These defenses he increased on subsequent days so that they might take the place of a wall as a barrier against the foe, and that he might not be obliged to fight against his will. Meanwhile the younger daughter of King Ptolemy, hoping to have the vacated tenure of the throne, removed herself from the palace to join Achillas and began to conduct the war with him. But there quickly arose a controversy between them about the leadership, an event which increased the bounties to the soldiers, for each strove separately to win their favor by large sacrifices. While this was going on among the enemy, Pothinus, the young king's tutor and controller of the kingdom, in Caesar's part of the town, while sending messengers to Achillas and exhorting him not to slacken in the business nor to fail in spirit, was slain by Caesar, his messengers having been informed against and arrested. This was the beginning of the Alexandrian war.

From Julius Caesar, *Civil War*, book 3 of *The Civil Wars* (London: William Heinemann, 1914), pp. 102–12, 339–59.

CAESAR MEETS CLEOPATRA

As for the war in Egypt, some say that it was not necessary, but due to Caesar's passion for Kleopatra, and that it was inglorious and full of peril for him. But others blame the king's party for it, and especially the eunuch Potheinos, who had most influence at court, and had recently killed Pompey; he had also driven Kleopatra from the country, and was now secretly plotting against Caesar. On this account they say that from this time on Caesar passed whole nights at drinking parties in order to protect himself. But in his open acts also Potheinos was unbearable, since he said and did many things that were invidious and insulting to Caesar. For instance, when the soldiers had the oldest and worst grain measured out to them, he bade them put up with it and be content, since they were eating what belonged to others; and at the state suppers he used wooden and earthen dishes, on the ground that Caesar had taken all the gold and silver ware in payment of a debt. For the father of the present king owed Caesar seventeen million five hundred thousand drachmas, of which Caesar had formerly remitted a part to his children, but now demanded payment of ten millions for the support of his army. When, however, Potheinos bade him go away now and attend to his great affairs, assuring him that later he would get his money with thanks, Caesar replied that he had no need whatever of Egyptians as advisers and secretly sent for Kleopatra from the country.

So Kleopatra, taking only Apollodoros the Sicilian from among her friends, embarked in a little skiff and landed at the palace when it was already getting dark; and as it was impossible to escape notice otherwise, she stretched herself at full length inside a bed-sack, while Apollodoros tied the bed-sack up with a cord and carried it indoors to Caesar. It was by this device of Kleopatra's, it is said, that Caesar was first captivated, for she showed herself to be a bold coquette, and succumbing to the charm of further intercourse with her, he reconciled her to her brother on the basis of a joint share with him in the royal power. Then, as everybody was feasting to celebrate the reconciliation, a slave of Caesar's, his barber, who left nothing unscrutinized, owing to a timidity in which he had no equal, but kept his ears open and was here, there, and everywhere, perceived that Achillas the general and Potheinos the eunuch were hatching a plot against Caesar. After Caesar had found them out, he set a guard about the banqueting-hall, and put Potheinos to death; Achillas, however, escaped to his camp, and raised about Caesar a war grievous and difficult for one who was defending himself with so few followers against so large a city and army. In this war, to begin with, Caesar encountered the peril of being shut off from water, since the canals were dammed up by the enemy; in the second place, when the enemy tried to cut off his fleet, he was forced to repel the danger by using fire, and this spread from the dockyards and destroyed the great library; and thirdly, when a battle arose at Pharos, he sprang from the mole into a small boat and tried to go to the aid of his men in their struggle, but the Egyptians sailed up against him from every side so that he threw himself into the sea and with great difficulty escaped by swimming. At this time, too, it is said that he was holding many papers in his hand and would not let them go, though missiles were flying at him and he was immersed in the sea but held them above water with one hand and swam with the other; his little boat had been sunk at the outset. But finally, after the king had gone away to the enemy, he marched against him and conquered him in a battle where many fell and the king himself disappeared. Then, leaving Kleopatra on the throne of Egypt (a little later she had a son by him whom the Alexandrians called Kaisarion), he set out for Syria.

From Plutarch, *Life of Caesar*, *Plutarch's Lives*, trans. Bernadotte Perrin (London: William Heinemann, 1919), pp. 555–60.

The Alexandrian War

When the Alexandrian war flared up, Caesar summoned every fleet from Rhodes and Syria and Cilicia; from Crete he raised archers, and cavalry from Malchus, king of the Nabataeans, and ordered artillery to be procured, grain dispatched, and auxiliary troops mustered from every quarter. Meanwhile the entrenchments were daily extended by additional works, and all those sectors of the town which appeared to be not strong enough were provided with shelters and mantlets; battering-rams, moreover, were introduced from one building into the next through holes, and the entrenchments were extended to cover all the ground laid bare by demolitions or gained by force of arms. For Alexandria is well-nigh fireproof, because buildings contain no wooden joinery and are held together by an arched construction and are roofed with rough-cast or tiling. Caesar was particularly anxious that, by bringing to bear his siege works and pent-houses, he should isolate from the rest of the city that narrowest part of the town which was most constricted by the barrier of marshland lying to the south; his object being first that, since his army was divided between two sectors of the city, it should be controlled by a single strategy and command; secondly, that if they got into difficulties in one sector of the town, assistance and support could be brought from the other sector. But above all his object was to secure himself abundance of water and fodder; of which, as regards the former, he had but a scanty supply, and, as regards the latter, no stocks whatever; and the marshland could afford him bountiful supplies of both.

Not indeed that this occasioned any hesitation or delay on the part of the Alexandrians in concerting their measures. They had in fact dispatched emissaries and recruiting officers throughout the entire length and breadth of the territory and kingdom of Egypt for the purpose of holding a levy, and had conveyed into the town a large quantity of weapons and artillery and mustered a countless host. In the city too, no less, vast arms factories had been established. They had, moreover, armed the adult slaves, and these the wealthier owners furnished with their daily food and pay. The numerous force they deployed to guard the fortifications of outlying areas; while they kept their veteran cohorts unemployed in the most frequented quarters of the city so that, no matter in what district fighting occurred, they could be thrown in as fresh and lusty reinforcements. All the streets and alleys were walled off by a triple barricade, built of rectangular stone blocks and not less than forty feet high; while as for the lower quarters of the city, these were fortified with very lofty towers, each ten stories high. Besides these there were other towers which they had contrived—mobile ones of the like number of stories; and these, being mounted on wheels with ropes and draught animals attached, they moved along the level streets to any area they saw fit.

Highly productive and abundantly supplied as it was, the city furnished equipment of all kinds. The people themselves were clever and very shrewd, and no sooner had they seen what was being done by us than they would reproduce it with such cunning that it seemed it was our men who had copied their works. Much also they invented on their own account, and kept assailing our entrenchments while simultaneously defending their own. In their councils and public meetings the arguments which their leaders kept driving home were as follows: "the Roman people were gradually acquiring a habit of seizing that kingdom; a few years earlier Aulus Gabinius had been in Egypt with an army; Pompey too had resorted thither in his flight; Caesar had now come with his forces, and the death of Pompey had had no effect in dissuading Caesar from staying on among them. If they failed to drive him out, their kingdom would become a Roman province: and this driving out they must do betimes; for cut off as he now was by storms owing to the season of the year, he could not receive reinforcements from overseas."

Meanwhile a quarrel had arisen—as related above—between Achillas, who commanded the veteran army, and Arsinoe, the younger daughter of king Ptolemey; and with each party plotting against the other and anxious to obtain the supreme power for himself, Arsinoe, acting through the eunuch Ganymedes, her tutor, struck the first blow and killed Achillas. After his murder she herself exercised complete control without any consort or guardian, while the army was entrusted to Ganymedes. On undertaking this duty the latter increased the soldiers' bounty and performed the rest of his functions with consistent thoroughness.

Practically the whole of Alexandria is undermined with subterranean conduits running from the Nile, by which water is conducted into private houses; which water in course of time gradually settles down and becomes clear. This is what is normally used by the owners of mansions and their households; for what the Nile brings down is so muddy and turbid that it gives rise to many different diseases: yet the rank and file of the common sort are perforce content with the latter, inasmuch as there is not one natural spring in the whole city. The main stream in question, however, was in that quarter of the city, which was held by the Alexandrians. This circumstance suggested to Ganymedes the possibility that the water supply could be cut off from our troops; who, posted as they were in various quarters of the town to guard our entrenchments, were using water drawn from conduits and cisterns in private buildings.

Ganymedes tries to force Caesar to surrender by fouling the drinking water in the portions of Alexandria he controlled with salt water. Caesar defeats the Egyptian forces in a naval battle in Alexandria harbor.

So shattered were the Alexandrians by this reverse—for they saw that now it was not the bravery of combat troops but the seamanship of sailors that had caused their defeat—that they scarcely trusted their ability to defend themselves from the buildings, from which, as well as from their higher positions, they derived support, and used all their timber in building barricades, fearing as they did that our fleet would attack them even ashore. Nevertheless, after Ganymedes had declared in the council that he would not only make good the losses they had sustained but also increase the number of their ships, their hopes and confidence ran high and they began to repair their old ships and to devote greater care and more earnest attention to this matter. And though they had lost more than a hundred and ten warships in the harbor and docks, yet they did not abandon the idea of re-equipping their fleet. They saw in fact that neither troop reinforcements nor supplies could be conveyed to Caesar if they themselves had a strong fleet; apart from which, the men of the city and the coastal district, seamen as they were and trained as such from boyhood by daily practice, were anxious to resort to this their natural and native gift, and were aware how successful they had been with their humble little vessels. Consequently they threw themselves whole-heartedly into the task of equipping a fleet.

There were guardships posted at all the mouths of the Nile to levy customs dues, and in secret royal dockyards there were old ships, which had not seen service afloat for many years. These last they proceeded to repair, while the guardships they recalled to Alexandria. There was a shortage of oars: the roofs of colonnades, gymnasia and public buildings were dismantled, and their beams made to serve as oars. In one case it was natural ingenuity that helped to bridge the gap, in another the city's resources. In fine it was no lengthy voyaging for which they were preparing; but perceiving that the conflict must take place in the harbor itself they obeyed the dictates of the moment. In a few days, therefore, they surprised everyone by completing 22 quadriremes and 5 quinqueremes, to which they added a considerable number of smaller, open craft; and then, after trying out in the harbor by rowing what each of them could do, they manned them with suitable troops and prepared themselves at all points for the conflict. Caesar had 9 Rhodian ships (10 had been sent, but one had been lost during a voyage, on the coast of Egypt), 8 Pontic, 5 Lycian and 12 from Asia. These included 10 quinqueremes and quadriremes, while the rest were smaller craft and most of them un-decked. None the less, though informed of the enemies' forces, Caesar proceeded with his preparations for an action, confident in the valor of his troops.

Caesar defeats the Egyptian forces in a second naval battle in Alexandria harbor.

The Alexandrians saw that the Romans were heartened by successes and stimulated by reverses, nor were they aware of any third vicissitude of war which could make them yet more steadfast. And so, whether it was they were warned by the king's friends who were in Caesar's camp, or whether they were acting on some previous plan of their own made known to the king by secret dispatches and approved by him,—we can only guess at their motive—they sent envoys to Caesar requesting him to release the king and allow him to go over to his own side. "The whole population," they said, "being tired and wearied of the girl, of the delegation of the kingship, and of the utterly remorseless tyranny of Ganymedes, were ready to do the king's bidding; and if, at his instance, they were to enter into a loyal friendship with Caesar, then no danger would intimidate or prevent the population from submitting."

Though Caesar was well aware that they were a deceitful race, always pretending something different from their real intentions, yet he decided that it was expedient to satisfy their plea for clemency, since, if their demands in any way reflected their feelings, then he believed the king would remain loyal when released; but if, on the other hand, they wanted to have the king to lead them with a view to waging the war—and that was more in keeping with their character—then he thought there would be greater honor and distinction for him in waging war against a king than against a motley collection of refugees. Accordingly, he urged the king to take thought for the kingdom of his fathers, to have pity on his most illustrious country, shamefully scarred as it was by fire and desolation, to recall his citizens to sanity first and then to preserve them therein, and to prove his loyalty to the Roman people and to Caesar, inasmuch as Caesar himself had such faith in him that he was sending him to join an enemy under arms. Then, grasping his right hand in his own, Caesar made to take leave of the boy—already grown to manhood. But the royal mind, schooled in all the lessons of utter deceit, was loth to fall short of the customary standards of his race; and so with tears he proceeded to beseech Caesar to the opposite effect not to send him away: his very kingdom, he declared, was not more pleasing to him than the sight of Caesar. Checking the lad's tears, albeit not unmoved himself, Caesar declared that, if that was the way he felt, they would speedily be reunited, and so sent him back to his people. Like a horse released from the starting-gate and given his head, the king proceeded to wage war against Caesar so energetically that the tears he had shed at their conference seemed to have been tears of joy. Not a few of Caesar's officers and friends and many of the centurions and soldiers were delighted at this turn of events, inasmuch as Caesar's over-generosity had, they felt, been made fun of by the deceitful tricks of a boy. As if indeed it was merely generosity and not the most far-sighted strategy, which had led him to do it!

Roman reinforcements commanded by Mithridates of Pergamum enter Egypt. Ptolemy XIII is defeated in battles against Mithridates and Caesar and killed.

It is established that the king himself fled from the camp and then, after being taken aboard a ship along with a large number of his men who were swimming to the nearest ships, perished when as a result of the numbers the vessel capsized.

This signal victory, the outcome of a most speedy and successful action, filled Caesar with such confidence that he hastened with his cavalry to Alexandria by the nearest overland route, and entered it triumphantly by that quarter of the town which was held by the enemy garrison. Nor was he mistaken in his own conclusion that, as soon as they heard of that battle, the enemy would cease to think any longer in terms of war. On his arrival he reaped the well-earned fruits of valor and magnanimity; for the entire population of townsfolk threw down their arms, abandoned their fortifications, assumed that garb in which suppliants are used to placate tyrants with earnest prayers, and brought forth all the sacred emblems by the sanctity of which they had been wont to conjure the embittered and wrathful hearts of their kings; even so did they hasten to meet Caesar on his arrival and surrender themselves to him. Caesar took them formally under his protection and consoled them; then, passing through the enemy fortifications, he came to his own quarter of the town amid loud cheers of congratulation from his own troops, who rejoiced at the happy issue, not only of the war itself and the fighting, but also of his arrival under such circumstances.

Having made himself master of Egypt and Alexandria, Caesar appointed as kings those whose names Ptolemy had written down in his will with an earnest appeal to the Roman people that they should not be altered. The elder of the two boys—the late king—being now no more, Caesar assigned the kingdom to the younger one and to Cleopatra, the elder of the two daughters, who had remained his loyal adherent; whereas Arsinoe, the younger daughter, in whose name, as we have shown, Ganymedes had long been exercising an unbridled sway, he determined to remove from the realm, to prevent any renewed dissentions coming into being among factious folk before the dominion of the royal pair could be consolidated by the passage of time. The veteran Sixth legion he took away with him: all the others he left there, the more to bolster up the dominion of the said rulers, who could enjoy neither the affection of their people, inasmuch as they had remained throughout staunch friends of Caesar, nor the authority of a long-established reign, it being but a few days since they came to the throne. At the same time he deemed it conducive to the dignity of our empire and to public expediency that, if the rulers remained loyal, they should be protected by our troops: whereas if they proved ungrateful, those same troops could hold them in check. Having thus completed all his dispositions, he set off in person for Syria.

From Julius Caesar, *The Alexandrian War*, in *Alexandrian, African and Spanish Wars*, trans. A. G. Way (Cambridge, MA: Harvard University Press, 1955), pp. 11–65.

RELATIONS BETWEEN CLEOPATRA AND ANTONY FROM THEIR MEETING IN 40 B.C.E. TO THEIR DEATH IN 30 B.C.E.

At any rate, when Antony made his entry into Ephesus, women arrayed like Bacchanals, and men and boys like Satyrs and Pans, led the way before him, and the city was full of ivy and thyrsus-wands and harps and pipes and flutes, the people hailing him as Dionysus Carnivorous and Savage. For he took their property from well-born men and bestowed it on flatterers and scoundrels. From many, too, who were actually alive, men got their property by asking him for it on the plea that the owners were dead. The house of a man of Magnesia he gave to a cook, who, as we are told, had won reputation by a single supper. But finally, when he was imposing a second contribution on the cities, Hybreas, speaking in behalf of Asia, plucked up courage to say this: "If thou canst take a contribution twice in one year, thou hast power also to make summer for us twice, and harvest-time twice." These words were rhetorical, it is true, and agreeable to Antony's taste; but the speaker added in plain and bold words that Asia had given him two hundred thousand talents; "If," said he, "thou hast not received this money, demand it from those who took it; but if thou didst receive it, and hast it not, we are undone." This speech made a powerful impression upon Antony; for he was ignorant of most that was going on, not so much because he was of an easy disposition, as because he was simple enough to trust those about him.

For there was simplicity in his nature, and slowness of perception, though when he did perceive his errors he showed keen repentance, and made full acknowledgement to the very men who had been unfairly dealt with, and there was largeness both in his restitution to the wronged and in his punishment of the wrong-doers. Yet he was thought to exceed due bounds more in conferring favors than in inflicting punishments. And his wantonness in mirth and jest carried its own remedy with it. For a man might pay back his jests and insolence, and he delighted in being laughed at no less than in laughing at others. And this vitiated most of his undertakings. For he could not believe that those who used bold speech in jest could flatter him in earnest, and so was easily captivated by their praises, not knowing that some men would mingle bold speech, like a piquant sauce, with flattery, and thus would take away from flattery its cloying character. Such men would use their bold babbling over the cups to make their submissive yielding in matters of business seem to be the way, not of those who associate with a man merely to please him, but of those who are vanquished by superior wisdom.

Such, then, was the nature of Antony, where now as a crowning evil his love for Kleopatra supervened, roused and drove to frenzy many of the passions that were still hidden and quiescent in him, and dissipated and destroyed whatever good and saving qualities still offered resistance. And he was taken captive in this manner. As he was getting ready for the Parthian war, he sent to Kleopatra, ordering her to meet him in Cilicia in order to make answer to the charges made against her of raising and giving to Cassius much money for the war. But Delius, Antony's messenger, when he saw how Kleopatra looked, and noticed her subtlety and cleverness in conversation, at once perceived that Antony would not so much as think of doing such a woman any harm, but that she would have the greatest influence with him. He therefore resorted to flattery and tried to induce the Egyptian to go to Cilicia "decked out in fine array" (as Homer would say), and not to be afraid of Antony, who was the most agreeable and humane of commanders. She was persuaded by Delius, and judging by the proofs which she had had before this of the effect of her beauty upon Caius Caesar and Gnaeus the son of Pompey, she had hopes that she would more easily bring Antony to her feet. For Caesar and Pompey had known her when she was still a girl and inexperienced in affairs, but she was going to visit Antony at the very time when women have the most brilliant beauty and are at the acme of intellectual power. Therefore she provided herself with many gifts, much money, and such ornaments as high position and a prosperous kingdom made it natural for her to take; but she went putting her greatest confidence in herself, and in the charms and sorceries of her own person.

Though she received many letters of summons both from Antony himself and from his friends, she so despised and laughed the man to scorn as to sail up the river Kydnos in a barge with gilded poop, its sails spread purple, its rowers urging it on with silver oars to the sound of the flute blended with pipes and lutes. She herself reclined beneath a canopy spangled with gold, adorned like Venus in a painting, while boys like Loves in paintings stood on either side and fanned her. Likewise also the fairest of her serving-maidens, attired like Nereïds and Graces, were stationed, some at the rudder-sweeps, and others at the reefing-ropes. Wondrous odors from countless incense-offerings diffused themselves along the river-banks. Of the inhabitants, some accompanied her on either bank of the river from its very mouth, while others went down from the city to behold the sight. The throng in the market place gradually streamed away, until at last Antony himself, seated on his tribunal, was left alone. And a rumor spread on every hand that Venus was come to revel with Bacchus for the good of Asia.

Antony sent, therefore, and invited her to supper; but she thought it meet that he should rather come to her. At once, then, wishing to display his complacency and friendly feelings, Antony obeyed and went. He found there a preparation that beggared description, but was most amazed at the multitude of lights. For, as we are told, so many of these were let down and displayed on all sides at once, and they were arranged and ordered with so many inclinations and adjustments to each other in the form of rectangles and circles, that few sights were so beautiful or so worthy to be seen as this.

On the following day Antony feasted her in his turn, and was ambitious to surpass her splendor and elegance, but in both regards he was left behind, and vanquished in these very points, and was first to rail at the meagerness and rusticity of his own arrangements. Kleopatra observed in the jests of Antony much of the soldier and the common man, and adopted this manner also towards him, without restraint now, and boldly. For her beauty, as we are told, was in itself not altogether incomparable, nor such as to strike those who saw her; but converse with her had an irresistible charm, and her presence, combined with the persuasiveness of her discourse and the character which was somehow diffused about her behavior towards others, had something stimulating about it. There was sweetness also in the tones of her voice; and her tongue, like an instrument of many strings, she could readily turn to whatever language she pleased, so that in her interviews with Barbarians she very seldom had need of an interpreter, but made her replies to most of them herself and unassisted, whether they were Ethiopians, Trogodytes, Hebrews, Arabians, Syrians, Medes or Parthians. Nay, it is said that she knew the speech of many other peoples also, although the kings of Egypt before her had not even made an effort to learn the native language, and some actually gave up their Macedonian dialect.

Accordingly, she made such booty of Antony that, while Fulvia his wife was carrying on war at Rome with Caesar in defense of her husband's interests, and while a Parthian army was hovering about Mesopotamia (over this country the generals of the king had appointed Labienus Parthian commander-in-chief, and were about to invade Syria), he suffered her to hurry him off to Alexandria. There, indulging in the sports and diversions of a young man of leisure, he squandered and spent upon pleasures that which Antiphon calls the most costly outlay, namely, time. For they had an association called The Inimitable Livers, and every day they feasted one another, making their expenditures of incredible profusion. At any rate, Philotas, the physician of Amphissa, used to tell my grandfather, Lamprias, that he was in Alexandria at the time, studying his profession, and that having got well acquainted with one of the royal cooks, he was easily persuaded by him (young man that he was) to take a view of the extravagant preparations for a royal supper. Accordingly, he was introduced into the kitchen, and when he saw all the other provisions in great abundance, and eight wild boars a-roasting, he expressed his amazement at what must be the number of guests. But the cook burst out laughing and said: "The guests are not many, only about twelve; but everything that is set before them must be at perfection, and this an instant of time reduces. For it might happen that Antony would ask for supper immediately, and after a little while, perhaps, would postpone it and call for a cup of wine, or engage in conversation with some one. Wherefore," he said, "not one, but many suppers are arranged; for the precise time is hard to hit." This tale, then, Philotas used to tell; and he said also that as time went on he became one of the medical attendants of Antony's oldest son, whom he had of Fulvia, and that he usually supped with him at his house in company with the rest of his comrades, when the young man did not sup with his father. Accordingly, on one occasion, as a physician was making too bold and giving much annoyance to them as they supped, Philotas stopped his mouth with some such sophism as the: "To the patient who is somewhat feverish cold water must be given; but everyone who has a fever is somewhat feverish; therefore to everyone who has a fever cold water should be given." The fellow was confounded and put to silence, whereat Antony's son was delighted and said with a laugh: "All this I bestow upon thee, Philotas," pointing to a table covered with a great many large beakers. Philotas acknowledged his good intentions, but was far from supposing that a boy so young had the power to give away so much. After a little while, however, one of the slaves brought the beakers to him in a sack, and bade him put his seal upon it. And when Philotas protested and was afraid to take them, "You miserable man," said the fellow, "why hesitate? Don't you know that the giver is the son of Antony, and that he has the right to bestow so many golden vessels? However, take my advice and exchange them all with us for money; since perchance the boy's father might miss some of the vessels, which are of ancient workmanship and highly valued for their art." Such details, then, my grandfather used to tell me, Philotas would recount at every opportunity.

But Kleopatra, distributing her flattery, not into the four forms of which Plato speaks, but into many, and ever contributing some fresh delight and charm to Antony's hours of seriousness or mirth, kept him in constant tutelage, and released him neither night nor day. She played at dice with him, drank with him, hunted with him, and watched him as he exercised himself in arms; and when by night he would station himself at the doors or windows of the common folk and scoff at those within, she would go with him on his round of mad follies, wearing the garb of a serving maiden. For Antony also would try to array himself like a servant. Therefore he always reaped a harvest of abuse, and often of blows, before coming back home; though most people suspected who he was. However, the Alexandrians took delight in their graceful and cultivated way; they liked him, and said that he used the tragic mask with the Romans, but the comic mask with them.

Now, to recount the greater part of his boyish pranks would be great nonsense. One instance will suffice. He was fishing once, and had bad luck, and was vexed at it because Kleopatra was there to see. He therefore ordered his fishermen to dive down and secretly fasten to his hook some fish that had been previously caught, and pulled up two or three of them. But the Egyptian saw through the trick, and pretending to admire her lover's skill, told her friends about it, and invited them to be spectators of it the following day. So great numbers of them got into the fishing boats, and when Antony had let down his line, she ordered one of her own attendants to get the start of him by swimming onto his hook and fastening on it a salted Pontic herring. Antony thought he had caught something, and pulled it up, whereupon there was great laughter, as was natural, and Kleopatra said: "Imperator, hand over thy fishing-rod to the fishermen of Pharos and Canopus; thy sport is the hunting of cities, realms, and continents."

Antony goes to Italy in 40 B.C.E. Confrontation between him and Octavian is avoided. The Second Triumvirate is reorganized to the advantage of Octavian. Peace between him and Antony is sealed by the marriage of Antony and his sister Octavia.

On the voyage, however, he picked up his (sc. Antony's) friends who were in flight from Italy, and learned from them that Fulvia had been to blame for the war, being naturally a meddlesome and headstrong woman, and hoping to draw Antony away from Kleopatra in case there should be a disturbance in Italy. It happened, too, that Fulvia, who was sailing to meet him, fell sick and died at Sicyon. Therefore there was even more opportunity for a reconciliation with Caesar (sc: Octavian). For when Antony reached Italy, and Caesar manifestly intended to make no charges against him, and Antony himself was ready to put upon Fulvia the blame for whatever was charged against himself, the friends of the two men would not permit any examination of the proffered excuse, but reconciled them, and divided up the empire, making the Ionian sea a boundary, and assigning the East to Antony, and the West to Caesar; they also permitted Lepidus to have Africa, and arranged that, when they did not wish for the office themselves, the friends of each should have the consulship by turns.

These arrangements were thought to be fair, but they needed a stronger security, and this security Fortune offered. Octavia was a sister of Caesar, older than he, though not by the same mother; for she was the child of Ancharia, but he, by a later marriage, of Atia. Caesar was exceedingly fond of his sister, who was, as the saying is, a wonder of a woman. Her husband, Caius Marcellus, had died a short time before, and she was a widow. Antony, too, now that Fulvia was gone, was held to be a widower, although he did not deny his relations with Kleopatra; he would not admit, however, that she was his wife, and in this matter his reason was still battling with his love for the Egyptian. Everybody tried to bring about this marriage. For they hoped that Octavia, who, besides her great beauty, had intelligence and dignity, when united to Antony and beloved by him, as such a woman naturally must be, would restore harmony and be their complete salvation. Accordingly, when both men were agreed, they went up to Rome and celebrated Octavia's marriage, although the law did not permit a woman to marry before her husband had been dead ten months. In this case, however, the senate passed a decree remitting the restriction in time.

Antony's generals defeat Parthian raids while Antony remains in Italy with Octavia, who bears him two daughters. Preparations are made for his great Parthian campaign.

But the dire evil which had been slumbering for a long time, namely, his passion for Kleopatra, which men thought had been charmed away and lulled to rest by better considerations, blazed up again with renewed power as he drew near to Syria. And finally, like the stubborn and unmanageable beast of the soul, of which Plato speaks, he spurned away all saving and noble counsels and sent Fonteius Capito to bring Cleopatra to Syria. And when she was come, he made her a present of no slight or insignificant addition to her dominions, namely, Phoenicia, Coele Syria,

Cyprus, and a large part of Cilicia; and still further, the balsam-producing part of Judaea, and all that part of Arabia Nabataea which slopes toward the outer sea. These gifts particularly annoyed the Romans. And yet he made presents to many private persons of tetrarchies and realms of great peoples, and he deprived many monarchs of their kingdoms, as, for instance, Antigonus the Jew, whom he brought forth and beheaded, though no other king before him had been so punished. But the shamefulness of the honors conferred upon Kleopatra gave most offence. And he heightened the scandal by acknowledging his two children by her, and called one Alexander and the other Kleopatra, with the surname for the first of Sun, and for the other of Moon. However, since he was an adept at putting a good face upon shameful deeds, he used to say that the greatness of the Roman empire was made manifest, not by what the Romans received, but by what they bestowed; and that noble families were extended by the successive begettings of many kings. In this way, at any rate, he said, his own progenitor was begotten by Herakles, who did not confine his succession to a single womb, nor stand in awe of laws like Solon's for the regulation of conception, but gave free course to nature, and left behind him the beginnings and foundations of many families.

And now Phraates put Hyrodes his father to death and took possession of his kingdom, other Parthians ran away in great numbers, and particularly Monaeses, a man of distinction and power, who came in flight to Antony. Antony likened the fortunes of the fugitive to those of Themistokles, compared his own abundant resources and magnanimity to those of the Persian kings, and gave him three cities, Larissa, Arethusa, and Hierapolis, which used to be called Bambyce. But when the Parthian king made an offer of friendship to Monaeses, Antony gladly sent Monaeses back to him, determined to deceive Phraates with a prospect of peace, and demanding back the standards captured in the campaign of Crassus, together with such of his men as still survived. Antony himself, however, after sending Kleopatra back to Egypt, proceeded through Arabia and Armenia to the place where his forces were assembled, together with those of the allied kings.

These kings were very many in number, but the greatest of them all was Artavasdes, king of Armenia, who furnished six thousand horse and seven thousand foot. Here Antony reviewed his army. There were, of the Romans themselves, sixty thousand foot-soldiers, together with the cavalry classed as Roman, namely, ten thousand Iberians and Celts; of the other nations there were thirty thousand, counting alike horsemen and light-armed troops.

And yet we are told that all this preparation and power, which terrified even the Indians beyond Bactria and made all Asia quiver, was made of no avail to Antony by reason of Kleopatra. For so eager was he to spend the winter with her that he began the war before the proper time, and managed everything confusedly. He was not master of his own faculties, but, as if he were under the influence of certain drugs or of magic rites, was ever looking eagerly towards her, and thinking more of his speedy return than of conquering the enemy.

Antony campaigns unsuccessfully against the Parthians. After returning to Egypt, he makes plans for a new Armenian campaign.

But afterwards, when he once more invaded Armenia, and by many invitations and promises induced Artavasdes to come to him, Antony seized him, and took him in chains down to Alexandria, where he celebrated a triumph. And herein particularly did he give offence to the Romans, since he bestowed the honorable and solemn rites of his native country upon the Egyptians for Kleopatra's sake. This, however, took place at a later time.

But now, hastening on through much wintry weather, which was already at hand, and incessant snow-storms, he lost eight thousand men on the march. He himself, however, went down with a small company to the sea, and in a little place between Berytus and Sidon, called White Village, he waited for Kleopatra to come; and since she was slow in coming he was beside himself with distress, promptly resorting to drinking and intoxication, although he could not hold out long at table, but in the midst of the drinking would often rise or spring up to look out, until she put into port, bringing an abundance of clothing and money for the soldiers. There are some, however, who say that he received the clothing from Kleopatra, but took the money from his own private funds, and distributed it as a gift from her.

But at Rome Octavia was desirous of sailing to Antony, and Caesar gave her permission to do so, as the majority say, not as a favour to her, but in order that, in case she were neglected and treated with scorn, he might have plausible ground for war. When Octavia arrived at Athens, she received letters from Antony in which he bade her remain there and told her of his expedition. Octavia, although she saw through the pre-text and was distressed, nevertheless wrote Antony asking whither he would have the things sent which she was bringing to him. For she was bringing a great quantity of clothing for his soldiers, many beasts of bur-den, and money and gifts for the officers and friends about him; and be-sides this, two thousand picked soldiers equipped as praetorian cohorts with splendid armor. These things were announced to Antony by a cer-tain Niger, a friend of his who had been sent from Octavia, and he added such praises of her as was fitting and deserved.

But Kleopatra perceived that Octavia was coming into a contest at close quarters with her, and feared lest, if she added to the dignity of her character and the power of Caesar her pleasurable society and her assid-uous attentions to Antony, she would become invincible and get com-plete control over her husband. She therefore pretended to be passionately in love with Antony herself, and reduced her body by slen-der diet; she put on a look of rapture when Antony drew near, and one of faintness and melancholy when he went away. She would contrive to be often seen in tears, and then would quickly wipe the tears away and try to hide them, as if she would not have Antony notice them. And she practiced these arts while Antony was intending to go up from Syria to join the Mede. Her flatterers, too, were industrious in her behalf, and used to revile Antony as hard-hearted and unfeeling, and as the destroyer of a mistress who was devoted to him and him alone. For Octavia, they said, had married him as a matter of public policy and for the sake of her brother, and enjoyed the name of wedded wife; but Kleopatra, who was queen of so many people, was called Antony's beloved, and she did not shun this name nor disdain it, as long as she could see him and live with him; but if she were driven away from him she would not survive it. At last, then, they so melted and enervated the man that he became fearful lest Kleopatra should throw away her life, and went back to Alexandria, putting off the Mede until the summer season, although Parthia was said to be suffering from internal dissensions. However, he went up and brought the king once more into friendly relations, and after betrothing to one of his sons by Kleopatra one of the king's daughters who was still small, he returned, his thoughts being now directed towards the civil war.

As for Octavia, she was thought to have been treated with scorn, and when she came back from Athens Caesar ordered her to dwell in her own house. But she refused to leave the house of her husband, nay, she even entreated Caesar himself, unless on other grounds he had determined to make war upon Antony, to ignore Antony's treatment of her, since it was an infamous thing even to have it said that the two greatest imperators in the world plunged the Romans into civil war, the one out of passion for, and the other out of resentment in behalf of, a woman. . . . Without meaning it, however, she was damaging Antony by this conduct of hers; for he was hated for wronging such a woman. He was hated, too, for the distribution, which he made to his children in Alexandria; it was seen to be theatrical and arrogant, and to evince hatred of Rome. For after filling the gymnasium with a throng and placing on a tribunal of silver two thrones of gold, one for himself and the other for Kleopatra, and other lower thrones for his sons, in the first place he declared Kleopatra Queen of Egypt, Cyprus, Libya, and Coele Syria, and she was to share her throne with Caesarion. Caesarion was believed to be a son of the former Caesar, by whom Kleopatra was left pregnant. In the second place, he proclaimed his own sons by Kleopatra Kings of Kings, and to Alexander he allotted Armenia, Media and Parthia (when he should have subdued it), to Ptolemy Phoenicia, Syria, and Cilicia. At the same time he also produced his sons, Alexander arrayed in Median garb, which included a tiara and upright head-dress, Ptolemy in boots, short cloak, and broad-brimmed hat surmounted by a diadem. For the latter was the dress of the kings who followed Alexander, the former that of Medes and Armenians. And when the boys had embraced their parents, one was given a bodyguard of Armenians, the other of Macedonians. Kleopatra, indeed, both then and at other times when she appeared in public, assumed a robe sacred to Isis, and was addressed as the New Isis.

By reporting these things to the senate and by frequent denunciations before the people Caesar tried to inflame the multitude against Antony. Antony, too, kept sending counter-accusations against Caesar. The chief accusations which he made were, in the first place, that after taking Sicily away from Pompey, Caesar had not assigned a part of the island to him; in the second place, that after borrowing ships from him for the war he had kept them for himself; thirdly, that after ejecting his colleague Lepidus from office and degrading him, he was keeping for himself the army, the territory, and the revenues which had been assigned to Lepidus; finally that he had distributed almost all Italy in allotments, to his own soldiers, and had left nothing for the soldiers of Antony. To these charges Caesar replied by saying that he had deposed Lepidus from office because he was abusing it, and as for what he had acquired in war, he would share it with Antony whenever Antony, on his part, should share Armenia with him; and Antony's soldiers had no claim upon Italy, since they had Media and Persia, which countries they had added to the Roman dominion by their noble struggles under their imperator.

Antony heard of this while he was tarrying in Armenia; and at once he ordered Canidius to take sixteen legions and go down to the sea. But he himself took Kleopatra with him and came to Ephesus. It was there that his naval force was coming together from all quarters, eight hundred ships of war with merchant vessels, of which Kleopatra furnished two hundred, besides twenty thousand talents, and supplies for the whole army during the war. But Antony, listening to the advice of Domitius and sundry others, ordered Kleopatra to sail to Egypt and there await the result of the war. Kleopatra, however, fearing that Octavia would again succeed in putting a stop to the war, persuaded Canidius by large bribes to plead her cause with Antony, and to say that it was neither just to drive away from the war a woman whose contributions to it were so large, nor was it for the interest of Antony to dispirit the Egyptians, who formed a large part of his naval force; and besides, it was not easy to see how Kleopatra was inferior in intelligence to anyone of the princes who took part in the expedition, she who for a long time had governed so large a kingdom by herself, and by long association with Antony had learned to manage large affairs. These arguments (since it was destined that everything should come into Caesar's hands) prevailed; and with united forces they sailed to Samos and there made merry. . . .

When these festivities were over, Antony gave the dramatic artists Priene as a place for them to dwell, and sailed himself to Athens, where sports and theatres again engaged him. Kleopatra, too, jealous of Octavia's honors in the city (for Octavia was especially beloved by the Athenians), tried by many splendid gifts to win the favor of the people. So the people voted honors to her, and sent a deputation to her house carrying the vote, of whom Antony was one, for was he not a citizen of Athens? And standing in her presence he delivered a speech in behalf of the city. To Rome, however, he sent men who had orders to eject Octavia from his house. And we are told that she left it taking all his children with her except his eldest son by Fulvia, who was with his father; she was in tears of distress that she herself also would be regarded as one of the causes of the war. But the Romans felt pity for Antony, not for her, and especially those who had seen Kleopatra and knew that neither in youthfulness nor beauty was she superior to Octavia.

Antony and Kleopatra make preparations for war against Octavian. Antony divorces Octavia and orders her to leave his house in Rome.

When Caesar heard of the rapidity and extent of Antony's preparations, he was much disturbed, lest he should be forced to settle the issue of the war during that summer. For he was lacking in many things, and people were vexed by the exactions of taxes. . . . Titius and Plancus, friends of Antony and men of consular rank, being abused by Kleopatra (for they had been most opposed to her accompanying the expedition) ran away to Caesar, and they gave him information about Antony's will, the contents of which they knew. This will was on deposit with the Vestal Virgins, and when Caesar asked for it, they would not give it to him; but if he wanted to take it, they told him to come and do so. So he went and took it; and to begin with, he read its contents through by himself; and marked certain reprehensible passages; then he assembled the senate and read it aloud to them, although most of them were displeased to hear him do so. For they thought it a strange and grievous matter that a man should be called to account while alive for what he wished to have done after his death. Caesar laid most stress on the clause in the will relating to Antony's burial. For it directed that Antony's body, even if he should die in Rome, should be borne in state through the forum and then sent away to Kleopatra in Egypt. Again, Calvisius, who was a companion of Caesar, brought forward against Antony the following charges also regarding his behavior towards Kleopatra: he had bestowed upon her the libraries from Pergamum, in which there were two hundred thousand volumes; at a banquet where there were many guests he had stood up and rubbed her feet, in compliance with some agreement and compact which they had made; he had consented to have the Ephesians in his presence salute Kleopatra as mistress; many times, while he was seated on his tribunal and dispensing justice to tetrarchs and kings, he would receive love-billets from her in tablets of onyx or crystal, and read them; and once when Furnius was speaking, a man of great worth and the ablest orator in Rome, Kleopatra was carried through the forum on a litter, and Antony, when he saw her, sprang up from his tribunal and forsook the trial, and hanging on to Kleopatra's litter escorted her on her way.

However, most of the charges thus brought by Calvisius were thought to be falsehoods; but the friends of Antony went about in Rome beseeching the people in his behalf, and they sent one of their number, Geminius, with entreaties that Antony would not suffer himself to be voted out of his office and proclaimed an enemy of Rome. But Geminius, after his voyage to Greece, was an object of suspicion to Kleopatra, who thought that he was acting in the interests of Octavia; he was always put upon with jokes at supper and insulted with places of no honor at table, but he endured all this and waited for an opportunity to confer with Antony. Once, however, at a supper, being bidden to tell the reasons for his coming, he replied that the rest of his communication required a sober head, but one thing he knew, whether he was drunk or sober, and that was all would be well if Kleopatra was sent off to Egypt. At this, Antony was wroth, and Kleopatra said: "You has done well, Geminius, to confess the truth without being put to the torture." Geminius, accordingly, after a few days, ran away to Rome. And Kleopatra's flatterers drove away many of the other friends of Antony also who could not endure their drunken tricks and scurrilities. Among these were Marcus Silanus and Delius the historian. And Delius says that he was also afraid of a plot against him by Kleopatra, of which Glaucus the physician had told him. For he had offended Kleopatra at supper by saying that while sour wine was served to them, Sarmentus, at Rome, was drinking Falernian. Now, Sarmentus was one of the youthful favorites of Caesar, such as the Romans call *deliciae*.

When Caesar had made sufficient preparations, a vote was passed to wage war against Kleopatra, and to take away from Antony the authority, which he had surrendered to a woman. And Caesar said in addition that Antony had been drugged and was not even master of himself, and that the Romans were carrying on war with Mardion the eunuch, and Potheinus, and Iras, and the tire-woman of Kleopatra, and Charmion, by whom the principal affairs of the government were managed.

Civil war breaks out between Antony and Octavian.

When the forces came together for the war, Antony had no fewer than five hundred fighting ships, among which were many vessels of eight and ten banks of oars, arrayed in pompous and festal fashion; he also had one hundred thousand infantry soldiers and twelve thousand horsemen. Of subject kings who fought with him, there were Bocchus the king of Libya, Tarcondemus the king of Upper Cilicia, Archelaüs of Cappadocia, Philadelphus of Paphlagonia, Mithridates of Commagene, and Sadalas of Thrace. These were with him, while from Pontus Polemon sent an army, and Malchus from Arabia, and Herod the Jew, besides Amyntas the king of Lycaonia and Galatia; the king of the Medes also sent an auxiliary force. Caesar had two hundred and fifty ships of war, eighty thousand infantry, and about as many horsemen as his enemies. Antony's authority extended over the country from the Euphrates and Armenia to the Ionian sea and Illyria; Caesar's over the country reaching from Illyria to the Western Ocean and from the ocean back to the Tuscan and Sicilian seas. Of Libya, the part extending opposite to Italy, Gaul, and Iberia as far as the pillars of Hercules, belonged to Caesar; the part extending from Cyrene as far as Armenia, to Antony.

But to such an extent, now, was Antony an appendage of the woman that although he was far superior on land, he wished the decision to rest with his navy, to please Kleopatra, and that too when he saw that for lack of crews his trierarchs were haling together out of long-suffering Greece wayfarers, mule-drivers, harvesters, and *ephebi*, and that even then their ships were not fully manned, but most of them were deficient and sailed wretchedly. Caesar's fleet, on the other hand, was perfectly equipped, and consisted of ships which had not been built for a display of height or mass, but were easily steered, swift, and fully manned.

Both sides make preparations for the decisive naval battle at Actium.

However, Kleopatra prevailed with her opinion that the war should be decided by the ships, although she was already contemplating flight, and was disposing her own forces, not where they would be helpful in winning the victory, but where they could most easily get away if the cause was lost. Moreover, there were two long walls extending down to the naval station from the camp, and between these Antony was wont to pass without suspecting any danger. But a slave told Caesar that it was possible to seize Antony as he went down between the walls, and Caesar sent men to lie in ambush for him. These men came near accomplishing their purpose, but seized only the man who was advancing in front of Antony, since they sprang up too soon; Antony himself escaped with difficulty by running.

When it had been decided to deliver a sea battle, Antony burned all the Egyptian ships except sixty; but the largest and best, from those having three to those having ten banks of oars, he manned, putting on board twenty thousand heavy-armed soldiers and two thousand archers.

The Battle of Actium

And now, as Agrippa was extending the left wing with a view to encircling the enemy, Publicola was forced to advance against him, and so was separated from the center. The center falling into confusion and engaging with Arruntius, although the sea-fight was still undecided and equally favourable to both sides, suddenly the sixty ships of Kleopatra were seen hoisting their sails for flight and making off through the midst of the combatants; for they had been posted in the rear of the large vessels, and threw them into confusion as they plunged through. The enemy looked on with amazement, seeing that they took advantage of the wind and made for Peloponnesus. Here, indeed, Antony made it clear to all the world that he was swayed neither by the sentiments of a commander nor of a brave man, nor even by his own, but, as someone in pleasantry said that the soul of the lover dwells in another's body, he was dragged along by the woman as if he had become incorporate with her and must go where she did. For no sooner did he see her ship sailing off than he forgot everything else, betrayed and ran away from those who were fighting and dying in his cause, got into a five-oared galley, where Alexas the Syrian and Scellius were his only companions, and hastened after the woman who had already ruined him and would make his ruin still more complete.

Kleopatra recognized him and raised a signal on her ship; so Antony came up and was taken on board, but he neither saw nor was seen by her. Instead, he went forward alone to the prow and sat down by himself in silence, holding his head in both hands. At this point, Liburnian ships were seen pursuing them from Caesar's fleet; but Antony ordered the ship's prow turned to face them, and so kept them off, except the ship of Eurykles the Laconian, who attacked vigorously, and brandished a spear on the deck as though he would cast it at Antony. And when Antony, standing at the prow, asked, "Who is this that pursues Antony?" the answer was, "I am Eurykles the son of Lachares, whom the fortune of Caesar enables to avenge the death of his father." Now, Lachares had been beheaded by Antony because he was involved in a charge of robbery.

However, Eurykles did not hit Antony's ship, but smote the other admiral's ship (for there were two of them) with his bronze beak and whirled her round, and one of the other ships also, which contained costly equipment for household use. When Eurykles was gone, Antony threw himself down again in the same posture and did not stir. He spent three days by himself at the prow, either because he was angry with Kleopatra, or ashamed to see her, and then put in at Taenarum. Here the women in Kleopatra's company at first brought them into a parley, and then persuaded them to eat and sleep together.

The rest of Antony's fleet and his land forces surrender to Octavian, who delays following Antony and Kleopatra to Egypt in order to settle affairs in Greece.

After Antony had reached the coast of Libya and sent Kleopatra forward into Egypt from Paraetonium, he had the benefit of solitude without end, roaming and wandering about with two friends, one a Greek, Aristocrates a rhetorician, and the other a Roman, Lucilius, about whom I have told a story elsewhere. He was at Philippi, and in order that Brutus might make his escape, pretended to be Brutus and surrendered himself to his pursuers. His life was spared by Antony on this account, and he remained faithful to him and steadfast up to the last crucial times. When the general to whom his forces in Libya had been entrusted brought about their defection, Antony tried to kill himself, but was prevented by his friends and brought to Alexandria. Here he found Kleopatra venturing upon a hazardous and great undertaking. The isthmus, namely, which separates the Red Sea from the Mediterranean Sea off Egypt and is considered to be the boundary between Asia and Libya, in the part where it is most constricted by the two seas and has the least width, measures three hundred furlongs. Here Kleopatra undertook to raise her fleet out of water and drag the ships across, and after launching them in the Arabian Gulf with much money and a large force, to settle in parts outside of Egypt, thus escaping war and servitude. But since the Arabians about Petra burned the first ships that were drawn up, and Antony still thought that his land forces at Actium were holding together, she desisted, and guarded the approaches to the country. And now Antony forsook the city and the society of his friends, and built for himself a dwelling in the sea at Pharos, by throwing a mole out into the water. Here he lived an exile

from men, and declared that he was contentedly imitating the life of
Timon, since, indeed, his experiences had been like Timon's; for he himself also had been wronged and treated with ingratitude by his friends,
and therefore hated and distrusted all mankind.

As for Antony, Canidius in person brought him word of the loss of his
forces at Actium, and he heard that Herod the Jew, with sundry legions
and cohorts, had gone over to Caesar, and that the other dynasts in like
manner were deserting him and nothing longer remained of his power
outside of Egypt. However, none of these things greatly disturbed him,
but, as if he gladly laid aside his hopes, that so he might lay aside his
anxieties also, he forsook that dwelling of his in the sea, which he called
Timoneum, and after he had been received into the palace by Kleopatra,
turned the city to the enjoyment of suppers and drinking-bouts and dis-
tributions of gifts, inscribing in the list of *ephebi* the son of Kleopatra and
Caesar, and bestowing upon Antyllus the son of Fulvia the *toga virilis*
without purple hem, in celebration of which, for many days, banquets
and revels and feastings occupied Alexandria. Kleopatra and Antony now
dissolved their famous society of Inimitable Livers, and founded another,
not at all inferior to that in daintiness and extravagant outlay, which they
called the society of Partners in Death. For their friends enrolled themselves as those who would die together, and passed the time delightfully
in a round of suppers. Moreover, Kleopatra was getting together collections of all sorts of deadly poisons, and she tested the painless working
of each of them by giving them to prisoners under sentence of death. But
when she saw that the speedy poisons enhanced the sharpness of death
by the pain they caused, while the milder poisons were not quick, she
made trial of venomous animals, watching with her own eyes as they were
set upon another.

She did this daily, tried them almost all; and she found that the bite
of the asp alone induced a sleepy torpor and sinking, where there was no
spasm or groan, but a gentle perspiration on the face, while the perceptive faculties were easily relaxed and dimmed, and resisted all attempts
to rouse and restore them, as is the case with those who are soundly
asleep.

At the same time they also sent an embassy to Caesar in Asia, Kleopatra asking the realm of Egypt for her children, and Antony requesting
that he might live as a private person at Athens, if he could not do so
in Egypt. But owing to their lack of friends and the distrust which they

felt on account of desertions, Euphronius, the teacher of the children, was sent on the embassy. For Alexas the Laodicean, who had been made known to Antony in Rome through Timagenes and had more influence with him than any other Greek, who had also been Kleopatra's most effective instrument against Antony and had overthrown the considerations arising in his mind in favor of Octavia, had been sent to keep Herod the king from apostasy; but after remaining there and betraying Antony he had the audacity to come into Caesar's presence, relying on Herod. Herod, however, could not help him, but the traitor was at once confined and carried in fetters to his own country, where he was put to death by Caesar's orders. Such was the penalty for his treachery, which Alexas paid to Antony while Antony was yet alive. Caesar would not listen to the proposals for Antony, but he sent back word to Kleopatra that she would receive all reasonable treatment if she either put Antony to death or cast him out. He also sent with the messengers one of his own freedmen, Thyrsus, a man of no mean parts, and one who would persuasively convey messages from a young general to a woman who was haughty and astonishingly proud in the matter of beauty. This man had longer interviews with Kleopatra than the rest, and was conspicuously honored by her, so that he roused suspicion in Antony, who seized him and gave him a flogging, and then sent him back to Caesar with a written message stating that Thyrsus, by his insolent and haughty airs, had irritated him, at a time when misfortunes made him easily irritated. "But if thou dost not like the thing," he said, "thou have my freedman Hipparchos; hang him up and give him a flogging, and we shall be quits." After this, Kleopatra tried to dissipate his causes of complaint and his suspicions by paying extravagant court to him; her own birthday she kept modestly and in a manner becoming to her circumstances, but she celebrated his with an excess of all kinds of splendor and costliness, so that many of those who were bidden to the supper came poor and went away rich. Meanwhile Caesar was being called home by Agrippa, who frequently wrote him from Rome that matters there greatly needed his presence.

Accordingly, the war was suspended for the time being; but when the winter was over, Caesar again marched against his enemy through Syria, and his generals through Libya. When Pelusium was taken there was a rumour that Seleukos had given it up, and not without the consent of Kleopatra; but Kleopatra allowed Antony to put to death the wife and children of Seleukos, and she herself, now that she had a tomb and monument built surpassingly lofty and beautiful, which she had erected near the temple of Isis, collected there the most valuable of the royal treasures, gold, silver, emeralds, pearls, ebony, ivory, and cinnamon; and besides all this she put there great quantities of torch-wood and tow, so that Caesar was anxious about the reason, and fearing lest the woman might become desperate and burn up and destroy this wealth, kept sending on to her vague hopes of kindly treatment from him, at the same time that he advanced with his army against the city. But when Caesar had taken up position near the hippodrome, Antony sallied forth against him and fought brilliantly and routed his cavalry, and pursued them as far as their camp. Then, exalted by his victory, he went into the palace, kissed Kleopatra, all armed as he was, and presented to her the one of his soldiers who had fought most spiritedly. Kleopatra gave the man as a reward of valor a golden breastplate and a helmet. The man took them, of course, and in the night deserted to Caesar.

And now Antony once more sent Caesar a challenge to single combat. But Caesar answered that Antony had many ways of dying. Then Antony, conscious that there was no better death for him than that by battle, determined to attack by land and sea at once. And at supper, we are told, he bade the slaves pour out for him and feast him more generously; for it was uncertain, he said, whether they would be doing this on the morrow, or whether they would be serving other masters, while he himself would be lying dead, a mummy and a nothing. Then, seeing that his friends were weeping at these words, he declared that he would not lead them out to battle, since from it he sought an honorable death for himself rather than safety and victory.

During this night, it is said, about the middle of it, while the city was quiet and depressed through fear and expectation of what was coming, suddenly certain harmonious sounds from all sorts of instruments were heard, and the shouting of a throng, accompanied by cries of Bacchic revelry and satyric leapings, as if a troop of revelers, making a great tumult, were going forth from the city; and their course seemed to lie about through the middle of the city toward the outer gate which faced the enemy, at which point the tumult became loudest and then dashed out. Those who sought the meaning of the sign were of the opinion that the god to whom Antony always most likened and attached himself was now deserting him.

At daybreak, Antony in person posted his infantry on the hills in front of the city, and watched his ships as they put out and attacked those of the enemy; and as he expected to see something great accomplished by them, he remained quiet. But the crews of his ships, as soon as they were near, saluted Caesar's crews with their oars, and on their returning the salute changed sides, and so all the ships, now united into one fleet, sailed up towards the city prows on. No sooner had Antony seen this than he was deserted by his cavalry, which went over to the enemy, and after being defeated with his infantry he retired into the city, crying out that he had been betrayed by Kleopatra to those with whom he waged war for her sake. But she, fearing his anger and his madness, fled for refuge into her tomb and let fall the drop-doors, which were made strong with bolts and bars; then she sent messengers to tell Antony that she was dead. Antony believed that message, and saying to himself, "Why doest thou longer delay, Antony? Fortune has taken away thy sole remaining excuse for clinging to life," he went into his chamber. Here, as he unfastened his breastplate and laid it aside, he said: "O Kleopatra, I am not grieved to be bereft of thee, for I shall straightway join thee; but I am grieved that such an imperator as I am has been found to be inferior to a woman in courage."

Now, Antony had a trusty slave named Eros. Him Antony had long before engaged, in case of need, to kill him, and now demanded the fulfillment of his promise. So Eros drew his sword and held it up as though he would smite his master, but then turned his face away and slew himself. And as he fell at his master's feet Antony said: "Well done, Eros! though you wast not able to do it thyself, you teachest me what I must do"; and running himself through the belly he dropped upon the couch. But the wound did not bring a speedy death. Therefore, as the blood ceased flowing after he had lain down, he came to himself and besought the bystanders to give him the finishing stroke. But they fled from the chamber, and he lay writhing and crying out, until Diomedes the secretary came from Kleopatra with orders to bring him to her in the tomb.

Having learned, then, that Kleopatra was alive, Antony eagerly ordered his servants to raise him up, and he was carried in their arms to the doors of her tomb. Kleopatra, however, would not open the doors, but showed herself at a window, from which she let down ropes and cords. To these Antony was fastened, and she drew him up herself, with the aid of the two women whom alone she had admitted with her into the tomb. Never, as those who were present tell us, was there a more piteous sight. Smeared with blood and struggling with death he was drawn up, stretching out his hands to her even as he dangled in the air. For the task was not an easy one for the women, and scarcely could Kleopatra, with clinging hands and strained face, pull up the rope, while those below called out encouragement to her and shared her agony. And when she had thus got him in and laid him down, she rent her garments over him, beat and tore her breasts with her hands, wiped off some of his blood upon her face, and called him master, husband, and imperator; indeed, she almost forgot her own ills in her pity for his. But Antony stopped her lamentations and asked for a drink of wine, either because he was thirsty, or in the hope of a speedier release. When he had drunk, he advised her to consult her own safety, if she could do it without disgrace, and among all the companions of Caesar to put most confidence in Proculeius, and not to lament him for his last reverses, but to count him happy for the good things that had been his, since he had become most illustrious of men, had won greatest power, and now had been not ignobly conquered, a Roman by a Roman.

Scarcely was he dead, when Proculeius came from Caesar. For after Antony had smitten himself and while he was being carried to Kleopatra, Dercetaeus, one of his body-guard, seized Antony's sword, concealed it, and stole away with it; and running to Caesar, he was the first to tell him of Antony's death, and showed him the sword all smeared with blood. When Caesar heard these tidings, he retired within his tent and wept for a man who had been his relation by marriage, his colleague in office and command, and his partner in many undertakings and struggles. Then he took the letters, which had passed between them, called in his friends, and read the letters aloud, showing how reasonably and justly he had written, and how rude and overbearing Antony had always been in his replies. After this, he sent Proculeius, bidding him, if possible, above all things to get Kleopatra into his power alive; for he was fearful about the treasures in her funeral pyre, and he thought it would add greatly to the glory of his triumph if she were led in the procession. Into the hands of Proculeius, however, Kleopatra would not put herself; but she conferred with him after he had come close to the tomb and stationed himself outside at a door, which was on a level with the ground. The door was strongly fastened with bolts and bars, but allowed a passage for the voice. So they conversed, Kleopatra asking that her children might have the kingdom, and Proculeius bidding her be of good cheer and trust Caesar in everything.

After Proculeius had surveyed the place, he brought back word to Caesar, and Gallus was sent to have another interview with the queen; and coming up to the door he purposely prolonged the conversation. Meanwhile Proculeius applied a ladder and went in through the window by which the women had taken Antony inside. Then he went down at once to the very door at which Kleopatra was standing and listening to Gallus, and he had two servants with him. One of the women imprisoned with Kleopatra cried out, "Wretched Kleopatra, thou art taken alive," whereupon the queen turned about, saw Proculeius, and tried to stab herself; for she had at her girdle a dagger such as robbers wear. But Proculeius ran swiftly to her, threw both his arms about her, and said: "O Kleopatra, thou art wronging both thyself and Caesar, by trying to rob him of an opportunity to show great kindness, and by fixing upon the gentlest of commanders the stigma of faithlessness and implacability." At the same time he took away her weapon, and shook out her clothing, to see whether she was concealing any poison. And there was also sent from Caesar one of his freedmen, Epaphroditos with injunctions to keep the queen alive by the strictest vigilance, but otherwise to make any concession that would promote her ease and pleasure.

And now Caesar himself drove into the city, and he was conversing with Areios the philosopher, to whom he had given his right hand, in order that Areios might at once be conspicuous among the citizens, and be admired because of the marked honor shown him by Caesar. After he had entered the gymnasium and ascended a tribunal there made for him, the people were beside themselves with fear and prostrated themselves before him, but he bade them rise up, and said that he acquitted the people of all blame, first, because of Alexander, their founder; second, because he admired the great size and beauty of the city; and third, to gratify his companion, Areios. This honor Caesar bestowed upon Areios, and pardoned many other persons also at his request. Among these was Philostratos, a man more competent to speak extempore than any sophist that ever lived, but he improperly represented himself as belonging to the school of the Academy.

Therefore Caesar, abominating his ways, would not listen to his entreaties. So Philostratos, having a long white beard and wearing a dark robe, would follow behind Areios, ever declaiming this verse: "A wise man will a wise man save, if wise he be." When Caesar heard of this, he pardoned him, wishing rather to free Areios from odium than Philostratos from fear.

As for the children of Antony, Antyllus, his son by Fulvia, was betrayed by Theodoros his tutor and put to death; and after the soldiers had cut off his head, his tutor took away the exceeding precious stone which the boy wore about his neck and sewed it into his own girdle; and though he denied the deed, he was convicted of it and crucified. Kleopatra's children, together with their attendants, were kept under guard and had generous treatment. But Caesarion, who was said to be Kleopatra's son by Julius Caesar, was sent by his mother, with much treasure, into India, by way of Ethiopia. There Rhodon, another tutor like Theodorus, persuaded him to go back, on the ground that Caesar invited him to take the kingdom. But while Caesar was deliberating on the matter, we are told that Areios said: "Not a good thing were a Caesar too many."

As for Caesarion, then, he was afterwards put to death by Caesar after the death of Kleopatra; but as for Antony, though many generals and kings asked for his body that they might give it burial, Caesar would not take it away from Kleopatra, and it was buried by her hands in sumptuous and royal fashion, such things being granted her for the purpose as she desired. But in consequence of so much grief as well as pain (for her breasts were wounded and inflamed by the blows she gave them) a fever assailed her, and she welcomed it as an excuse for abstaining from food and so releasing herself from life without hindrance. Moreover, there was a physician in her company of intimates, Olympos, to whom she told the truth, and she had his counsel and assistance in compassing her death, as Olympos himself testifies in a history of these events which he published. But Caesar was suspicious, and plied her with threats and fears regarding her children, by which she was laid low, as by engines of war, and surrendered her body for such care and nourishment as was desired.

After a few days Caesar himself came to talk with her and give her comfort. She was lying on a mean pallet-bed, clad only in her tunic, but sprang up as he entered and threw herself at his feet; her hair and face were in terrible disarray, her voice trembled, and her eyes were sunken. There were also visible many marks of the cruel blows upon her bosom; in a word, her body seemed to be no better off than her spirit. Nevertheless, the charm for which she was famous and the boldness of her beauty were not altogether extinguished, but, although she was in such a sorry plight, they shone forth from within and made themselves manifest in the play of her features. After Caesar had bidden her to lie down and had seated himself near her, she began a sort of justification of her course, ascribing it to necessity and fear of Antony; but as Caesar opposed and refuted her on every point, she quickly changed her tone and sought to move his pity by prayers, as one who above all things clung to life. And finally she gave him a list which she had of all her treasures; and when Seleukos, one of her stewards, showed conclusively that she was stealing away and hiding some of them, she sprang up, seized him by the hair, and showered blows upon his face. And when Caesar, with a smile, stopped her, she said: "But is it not a monstrous thing, O Caesar, that when thou hast deigned to come to me and speak to me though I am in this wretched plight, my slaves denounce me for reserving some women's adornments,—not for myself, indeed, unhappy woman that I am,—but that I may make trifling gifts to Octavia and thy Livia, and through their intercession find thee merciful and more gentle?" Caesar was pleased with this speech, being altogether of the opinion that she desired to live. He told her, therefore, that he left these matters for her to manage, and that in all other ways he would give her more splendid treatment than she could possibly expect. Then he went off, supposing that he had deceived her, but the rather deceived by her.

Now, there was a young man of rank among Caesar's companions, named Cornelius Dolabella. This man was not without a certain tenderness for Kleopatra; and so now, in response to her request, he secretly sent word to her that Caesar himself was preparing to march with his land forces through Syria, and had resolved to send off her and her children within three days. After Kleopatra had heard this, in the first place, she begged Caesar that she might be permitted to pour libations for Antony; and when the request was granted, she had herself carried to the tomb, and embracing the urn which held his ashes, in company with the women usually about her, she said: "Dear Antony, I buried thee but lately with hands still free; now, however, I pour libations for thee as a captive, and so carefully guarded that I cannot either with blows or tears disfigure this body of mine, which is a slave's body, and closely watched that it may grace the triumph over thee. Do not expect other honors or libations; these are the last from Kleopatra the captive. For though in life nothing could part us from each other, in death we are likely to change places; thou, the Roman, lying buried here, while I, the hapless woman, lie in Italy, and get only so much of thy country as my portion. But if indeed there is any might or power in the gods of that country (for the gods of this country have betrayed us), do not abandon thine own wife while she lives, nor permit a triumph to be celebrated over myself in my person, but hide and bury me here with thyself, since out of all my innumerable ills not one is so great and dreadful as this short time that I have lived apart from thee."

After such lamentations, she wreathed and kissed the urn, and then ordered a bath to be prepared for herself. After her bath, she reclined at table and was making a sumptuous meal. And there came a man from the country carrying a basket; and when the guards asked him what he was bringing there, he opened the basket, took away the leaves, and showed them that the dish inside was full of figs. The guards were amazed at the great size and beauty of the figs, whereupon the man smiled and asked them to take some; so they felt no mistrust and bade him take them in. After her meal, however, Kleopatra took a tablet, which was already written upon and sealed, and sent it to Caesar, and then, sending away all the rest of the company except her two faithful women, she closed the doors.

But Caesar opened the tablet, and when he found there lamentations and supplications of one who begged that he would bury her with Antony, he quickly knew what had happened. At first he was minded to go himself and give aid; then he ordered messengers to go with all speed and investigate. But the mischief had been swift. For though his messengers came on the run and found the guards as yet aware of nothing, when they opened the doors they found Kleopatra lying dead upon a golden couch, arrayed in royal state. And of her two women, the one called Iras was dying at her feet, while Charmion, already tottering and heavy-handed, was trying to arrange the diadem which encircled the queen's brow.

Then somebody said in anger: "A fine deed, this, Charmion!" "It is indeed most fine," she said, "and befitting the descendant of so many kings." Not a word more did she speak, but fell there by the side of the couch. It is said that the asp was brought with those figs and leaves and lay hidden beneath them, for thus Kleopatra had given orders, that the reptile might fasten itself upon her body without her being aware of it. But when she took away some of the figs and saw it, she said: "There it is, you see," and baring her arm she held it out for the bite. But others say that the asp was kept carefully shut up in a water jar, and that while Kleopatra was stirring it up and irritating it with a golden distaff it sprang and fastened itself upon her arm. But the truth of the matter no one knows; for it was also said that she carried about poison in a hollow comb and kept the comb hidden in her hair; and yet neither spot nor other sign of poison broke out upon her body. Moreover, not even was the reptile seen within the chamber, though people said they saw some traces of it near the sea, where the chamber looked out upon it with its windows. And some also say that Kleopatra's arm was seen to have two slight and indistinct punctures; and this Caesar also seems to have believed. For in his triumph an image of Kleopatra herself with the asp clinging to her was carried in the procession.

These, then, are the various accounts of what happened. But Caesar, although vexed at the death of the woman, admired her lofty spirit; and he gave orders that her body should be buried with that of Antony in splendid and regal fashion. Her women also received honorable interment by his orders. When Kleopatra died she was forty years of age save one, and had shared her power with Antony more than fourteen. Antony was fifty-six years of age, according to some, according to others, fifty-three. Now, the statues of Antony were torn down, but those of Kleopatra were left standing, because Archibios, one of her friends, gave Caesar two thousand talents, in order that they might not suffer the same fate as Antony's.

Antony left seven children by his three wives, of whom Antyllus, the eldest, was the only one who was put to death by Caesar; the rest were taken up by Octavia and reared with her own children. Kleopatra, the daughter of Kleopatra, Octavia gave in marriage to Juba, the most accomplished of kings, and Antony, the son of Fulvia, she raised so high that, while Agrippa held the first place in Caesar's estimation, and the sons of Livia the second, Antony was thought to be and really was third. By Marcellus Octavia had two daughters, and one son, Marcellus, whom Caesar made both his son and his son-in-law, and he gave one of the daughters to Agrippa. But since Marcellus died very soon after his marriage and it was not easy for Caesar to select from among his other friends a son-in-law whom he could trust, Octavia proposed that Agrippa should take Caesar's daughter to wife, and put away her own. First Caesar was persuaded by her, then Agrippa, whereupon she took back her own daughter and married her to young Antony, while Agrippa married Caesar's daughter. Antony left two daughters by Octavia, of whom one was taken to wife by Domitius Ahenobarbus, and the other, Antonia, famous for her beauty and discretion, was married to Drusus, who was the son of Livia and the step-son of Caesar. From this marriage sprang Germanicus and Claudius; of these, Claudius afterwards came to the throne, and of the children of Germanicus, Caius reigned with distinction, but for a short time only, and was then put to death with his wife and child, and Agrippina, who had a son by Ahenobarbus, Lucius Domitius, became the wife of Claudius Caesar. And Claudius, having adopted Agrippina's son, gave him the name of Nero Germanicus. This Nero came to the throne in my time. He killed his mother, and by his folly and madness came near subverting the Roman empire. He was the fifth in descent from Antony.

From Plutarch, *Life of Antony, Plutarch's Lives,* trans. Bernadotte Perrin (London: William Heinemann, 1920), pp. 187–333.

DOCUMENT 2
The Meaning of the Battle of Actium in Roman Eyes

With the defeat of Antony and Cleopatra's fleet in the Battle of Actium, Octavian's domination of the Roman empire was confirmed. A group of talented writers, who were his clients, provided the definitive interpretation of the significance of his victory for future generations of Romans. In the first selection, the poet Horace celebrates the return of peace and Rome's escape from Cleopatra's evil plans. In the second selection from Rome's national epic, the Aeneid, Horace's friend Virgil interprets the significance of the battle in the broad sweep of Roman history, viewing it as the decisive conflict between the sober values of Rome, championed by Octavian, and the corrupt values of the orient, represented by Egypt and Cleopatra.

Now is the time to drain the flowing bowl, now with unfettered foot to beat the ground with dancing, now with Salian feast to deck the couches of the gods, my comrades! Before this day it had been wrong to bring our Caecuban froth from ancient bins, while yet a frenzied queen was plotting ruin against the Capitol and destruction to the empire, with her polluted crew of creatures foul with lust—a woman mad enough to nurse the wildest hopes, and drunk with Fortune's favors. But the escape of scarce a single galley from the flames sobered her fury, and Caesar changed the wild delusions bred by Mareotic wine to the stern reality of terror, chasing her with his galleys, as she [Cleopatra] sped away from Italy, even as the hawk pursues the gentle dove, or the swift hunter follows the hare over the plains of snow-clad Thessaly, with purpose fixed to put in chains the accursed monster. Yet she, seeking to die a nobler death, showed for the dagger's point no woman's fear, nor sought to win with her swift fleet some secret shore; she even dared to gaze with serene face upon her fallen palace; courageous, too, to handle poisonous asps, that she might draw black venom to her heart, waxing as she resolved to die; scorning, in truth, the thought of being borne, a queen no longer, on hostile galleys to grace a glorious triumph—no cowardly woman she!

From Horace, *Odes* 1:37, in *The Odes and Epodes*, trans. C. E. Bennett (London: William Heinemann, 1914) pp. 99–101.

Amidst these scenes flowed wide the likeness of the swelling sea, all gold, but the blue water foamed with white billows, and round about dolphins, shining in silver, swept the seas with their tails in circles, and cleft the tide. In the center could be seen brazen ships with Actium's battle; one might see all Leucadia aglow with War's array, and the waves ablaze with gold. Here Augustus Caesar, leading Italians to strife, with peers and people, and the great gods of the Penates, stands on the lofty stern; his joyous brows pour forth a double flame, and on his head dawns his father's star. Elsewhere Agrippa with favoring winds and gods, high towering, leads his column; his brows gleam with the beaks of the naval crown, proud device of war. Here Antonius with barbaric might and varied arms, victor from the nations of the dawn and from the red sea, brings with him Egypt and the strength of the East and utmost Bactra; and there follows him (O shame!) his Egyptian wife.

All rush on at once, and the whole sea foams, torn up by the sweeping oars, and triple-pointed beaks. To the deep they speed; you would believe the Cyclades, uprooted, were floating on the sea, or that high mountains clashed with mountains; in such mighty ships the seamen assail the towered sterns. Flaming cloth and shafts of winged steel are showered from their hands; Neptune's fields redden with strange slaughter. In the midst the queen calls upon her hosts with their native cymbal, nor as yet casts back a glance at the twin snakes behind. Monstrous gods of every form and barking Anubis wield weapons against Neptune and

Venus and against Minerva. In the midst of the battle storms Mavors, embossed in steel, with the grim Furies from on high; and in torn robe Discord strides in joy; while Bellona follows her with bloody whip. Actian Apollo saw the sight, and from above was bending his bow; at that terror all Egypt and India, all Arabians, all Sabaeans, turned to flee.

The queen herself was seen to woo the winds, spread sail, and now, even now, fling loose the slackened sheets. Her, amid the carnage, the Lord of Fire had made pale at the coming of death, borne on by waves and the wind of Iapyx; while over against her was the mourning Nile, of mighty frame, opening wide his folds and with all his garments welcoming the defeated to his azure lap and sheltering streams.

From Virgil, *Aeneid* 8, lines 671–713, in *The Aeneid 7–12: The Minor Poems*, trans. H. R. Fairclough (London: William Heinemann, 1918), pp. 107–9.

DOCUMENT 3
The Administration of Ptolemaic Egypt: Ideal and Reality

The administration of Ptolemaic Egypt exemplifies the conflict between ideal and reality. The first selection is from an essay on the ideal administrator supposedly written by a senior financial official to a new district administrator. In it the author emphasizes the need for a administrator to be of upright character and to fairly implement government policy while being alert to the efforts of the kingdom's Egyptian subjects to evade their obligations. The second and third selections are from royal decrees that reveal how Ptolemaic government actually worked. The amnesty decree issued by Ptolemy VIII and Cleopatra II and Cleopatra III in 118 B.C.E. throws a bright light on widespread corruption by government officials and the efforts of the king to control it. The references to various kinds of illegal activities by officials in the decree of Cleopatra VII granting privileges to Quintus Cascellius demonstrates that the same problems continued right up to the end of Ptolemaic history. The final document in this section makes clear that these problems were not limited to the central government but were common even at the village level.

During your tours of inspection, try, while making your rounds, to encourage each individual and to make them bolder. Do this not only by word but also, if some of them lay a complaint against the village scribes or headmen concerning some matter pertaining to farming, look into it and, so far as you can, put an end to such situations. And when the sowing has been completed, it would not be a bad idea if you made a careful inspection; for, thus, you will accurately observe the sprouting, and you will easily identify the fields that have been improperly sown or not sown at all; and you will learn from this those who were careless and you will know if some have employed the seeds for other purposes. In addition, the sowing of the *nome* in accordance with the plan for planting is to be one of your prime concerns. And if some are suffering because of their rents or even have been completely ruined, do not allow this to be unexamined. Also, make a list of the oxen involved in farming, both royal and private, and exercise due care that the calves of the royal cattle, when they are ready to eat hay, are sent to the calf-rearing barns.

It is your responsibility also that the designated provisions are transported to Alexandria—of these we are sending you a list—on schedule, and not only in the proper amount, but also tested and suitable for consumption. Go also to the weaving sheds in which the linen is woven and take special care that as many as possible of the looms are in operation and that the weavers are completing the amount of fabric specified in the plan. If some are behind in their assigned work, let them be fined for each category the scheduled price. Moreover, to the end that the linen be usable and have the number of threads specified in the regulation, pay careful attention. As for looms that are not in operation, have all of them transported to the *nome* metropolis and stored in the storerooms under seal. Conduct an audit also of the revenues, if it is possible, village by village, and this seems to be not impossible if you zealously apply yourself to the task; but if not, then *toparchy* by *toparchy*, accepting in the audit with regard to money taxes only what has been deposited at the bank; and with regard to the grain taxes and oil produce what has been measured and received by the *sitologoi*. If there is any deficiency in these, compel the *toparchs* and the tax farmers to pay to the banks for arrears in the grain tax the price specified in the schedule and for arrears in the oil produce by wet measure according to each category. . . .

As the revenue from the pasture dues is among the most significant, it will be particularly increased if you conduct the census in the best way. The most suitable time for it is around the month of Mesore, for, at this time, because the whole land is covered by the flood waters, the herdsmen send their herds to the highest places, as they are unable to disperse them to other places. You should also take care that goods are not sold for more than the specified prices. As for those goods without set prices and for which the vendors may charge what they wish, examine this carefully and, having determined a moderate profit for the merchandise being sold, compel the [   ] make the disposition. . . .

Make a list also of the royal houses and of the gardens associated with them and who is supposed to care for each, and inform us. Further, it should be your concern also that affairs regarding the *machimoi* be handled in accordance with the memorandum which we drafted concerning persons who had absconded from their tasks and [   ] sailors in order that to [   ] the prisoners be confined until their transportation to Alexandria. Take particular care that no fraud occur or any other wrongful act, for it ought to be clearly understood by everyone living in the countryside and believed that all such matters have been corrected and that they are free from the former evil conditions, since no one has the power to do what he wishes but everything is being managed in the best way. Thus you will create security in the countryside and (increase) the revenues significantly. . . .

The reasons I sent you to the *nome*, I told you, but I thought it would be good also to send you a written copy of them in this memorandum. Afterwards, you should behave well and be upright in your duties, not become involved with bad company, avoid any involvement in corruption, believe that if you are not accused of such things, you will merit promotion, have this memorandum at hand and write concerning each matter as required.

From "'Take Particular Care That No Fraud Occur': The Ideal of Honest and Efficient Administration: P. Tebtunis 703." In Stanley M. Burstein, *The Hellenistic Age from the Battle of Ipsos to the Death of Kleopatra VII* (Cambridge: Cambridge University Press, 1985), pp. 128–29.

Col. I

King Ptolemy and Queen Kleopatra, the sister, and Queen Kleopatra, the Wife, pardon those subject to their rule, all of them, for errors, wrongful acts, accusations, condemnations, charges of all sorts up to the 9th of Pharmouthi of the 52nd year except those guilty of willful murder and sacrilege. They have given orders also that those who have fled because of being accused of theft and other charges shall return to their own homes and resume their former occupations, and that they shall recover whatever of their property still remains unsold from that which had been seized as security because of these matters.

COL. II

They have given orders also that all those having land allotments and all those in possession of sacred land and other released land, who have intruded into royal land and others who possess more land than is proper, having withdrawn from all excess they possess and having declared themselves and paid a year's rent in kind, shall be forgiven for the period up to year 51—and they shall have full possession.

COL. III

No one is to take away anything consecrated to the gods by force nor to apply forceful persuasion to the managers of the sacred revenues, whether villages or land or other sacred revenues, nor are taxes on associations or crowns or grain-taxes to be collected by anyone from property consecrated to the gods nor are the sacred lands to be placed under patronage on any pretext, but they are to allow them to be managed by the priests themselves.

COL. IV

They have given orders that the costs for the burial of Apis and Mnevis are to be sought from the royal treasury as also in the case of those who have been deified. Likewise, also the costs of the other sacred animals.

COL. VIII

They have given orders that *strategoi* and other officials are not to seize any of those living in the countryside for their private purposes nor are their animals to be requisitioned for any of their personal needs nor are their cattle to be seized nor are they to be forced to raise sacred animals or geese or birds or pigs or to furnish grain at a low price or in return for renewals of their leases nor to compel tasks to be performed by them as a gift on any pretext.

COL. IX

They have given orders also concerning suits of Egyptians against Greeks and concerning suits of Greeks against Egyptians or of Egyptians against Greeks of all categories except those of persons farming royal land and of those bound to government tasks and of others connected with the revenues, that those Egyptians who have made contracts in the Greek manner with Greeks shall be sued and sue before the *chrematistai*. All Greeks who make contracts in the Egyptian manner shall be sued before the *laokritai* in accordance with the laws of the country. The cases of Egyptians against Egyptians are not to be usurped by the *chrematistai*, but they are to allow them to be settled before the *laokritai* in accordance with the laws of the country.

From "Administrative Oppression in Ptolemaic Egypt: The Amnesty of 118 B.C.E." In Stanley M. Burstein, *The Hellenistic Age from the Battle of Ipsos to the Death of Kleopatra VII* (Cambridge: Cambridge University Press, 1985), pp. 139–40.

DECREE OF CLEOPATRA VII IN FAVOR OF QUINTUS CASCELLIUS (33 B.C.E.)

Received year 18 which is year 4, 26th day of Mecheir

To:
    We have granted to Quintus Cascellius and to his heirs the right to export annually ten thousand *artabas* of grain and to import five thousand amphoras of Coan wine without tax being levied by anyone or any other cost at all. We have also granted that all of his property in the country shall be exempt from taxes so that nothing will ever be exacted in any manner for the government administration or for the private account of us. . . . In addition his agricultural workers shall be exempt from personal service and taxes levied by anyone, nor shall they be liable for

occasional special levies in the *nomes* nor shall they be liable for civilian or military expenses. The animals used for agricultural work, beasts of burden, and boats used to transport grain shall in the same way be exempt from personal service, taxes, and seizure. Write to whomever it is appropriate in order that they may know and act accordingly.

Let it be so.

(Archival notation) 475

To Dioskourides, chief bodyguard of the king and *dioiketes*, from Harmais son of Marres, royal cultivator from Theadelphia of the Thernistos division of the Arsinoite nome. Because I am greatly wronged and chased from my home [   ] by Mesthasythmis the *komarch* of the village, I have fled to you to receive help. For in the 27th year, when I had been appointed by Mesthasythmis as *dekanos* of royal cultivators in the village, and he made a substantial *paralogeia* each year from the same cultivators [½] *artaba* of wheat per *aroura* and 90 drachmas of bronze, from which he was amassing it to be stolen. Appointing (?) along with me his own secretary, Pnepheros son of Petesouchos, for the *paralogeia* of the bronze, and Kollouthes son of Patis and Tothoes son of Papentpos his . . . for that of the wheat, to . . . everything in the month of Pachon to ship, namely the *half-artaba* of wheat per *aroura* and 85 drachmas of bronze.

And in the 28th year, a certain Seleukos who had made a complaint against him concerning the same *paralogeiai* and other taxes, was basely seized by Seleukos . . . their testimony from the documents which he had recovered. But when he fled to the Temple of Sarapis in the village because of his knowledge of these matters, the aforementioned Mesthasythmis did not . . . until . . . shook him down . . . all the documents concerning the affairs relating to Seleukos, 68 drachmas of silver. Similarly, in the payment which he made to the treasury . . . in the Temple of Sarapis in the village, from which were gathered a total of 500 *artabas* of wheat. And entering into the royal granary, he abstracted from the seed-grain on deposit there, from which . . . of mine alone 75 *artabas*, which he appropriated, with the rest of the remainder of the 500 *artabas*, which also had been exported for sale through Kollouthes and Thasos his mother and Kollouthis his wife.

Moreover, in the 29th year he compelled us to take charge of the same *paralogeia*, for a *half-artaba* and 50dr. of bronze for each *aroura*, which was exacted illegally through us and Thothoes son of Papentpos by the six-choinix measure of the village, and the wheat was stored in the houses of Limnaios and Leontomenes the 80-*aroura* settler, and the bronze money was turned over to Mesthasythmis himself. After this . . . in the 30th year, when documents arrived locally . . . and I informed Mesthasythmis . . . but after I sailed down to the city so as to sell the (produce?) from the previous (?), being bad by nature, he brought a charge against me and handed me over to the jail in Krokodilopolis. . . . He did not release me until he compelled me to . . . execute a cession in his favor of the royal land which I farm, along with the crop on it, until I paid him. Since he brought to the matter loss . . . , and in addition he confiscated the seed-grain lying in the royal granary to the amount of 150 *artabas*, in place of which . . . with many shortfalls, in addition to which . . . so that no loss would occur to the treasury. Entangled with an evil man, then, I set out for flight to the king and queen after explaining everything in writing. Taking policemen and his overseers with the same intention, he had the roads watched closely, wanting to drag me back to prison so that I could not sail down to the city and give testimony. Therefore, addressing . . . I ask that if you please you give orders to . . . my testimony about these things . . . and if this happens I shall have been helped. Farewell.

(Subscription) . . . let a written statement of the witnesses be sent from those present. Year 30, Choiak 22.

From "Extortion Racket Run by a Village Headman." In Roger S. Bagnall and Peter Derow, eds., *The Hellenistic Period: Historical Sources in Translation* (Oxford: Blackwell Publishing, 2004), pp. 159–60. Ellipses indicate incomplete text.

DOCUMENT 4
Cleopatra's Alexandria

The Greek geographer Strabo visited Alexandria in the late 20s B.C.E., *a little less than a decade after Cleopatra died. His brief description of the city provides essential evidence for Alexandria at the peak of its prosperity and prestige. Strabo, however, views Alexandria from a colonial perspective, considering only the Greek aspect of the city as significant and ignoring its Egyptian monuments. The second century* B.C.E. *author of the* Potter's Oracle *provides a radically different point of view, seeing Alexandria as the center of foreign rule and oppression. Like other exam-*

ples of the genre of prophetic texts, he paints a picture of Egypt under Ptolemaic Egypt as turned upside down. Nature and civil society are both dominated by the forces of evil. Justice will return only when Alexandria and its Greek inhabitants disappear and the gods return to Memphis and a true king rules in the ancient capital of Egypt.

The site of Alexandria is advantageous for many reasons. For the city is bounded by two seas, on the north by the so-called Egyptian sea and on the south by Lake Mareia, which is also called Mareotis. The Nile fills Lake Mareia through many canals from both the south and the sides. Through these canals many more goods are brought to Alexandria than arrive from the sea, so that the lakeside harbor is richer than that on the sea, and by it more goods are exported from Alexandria than are imported into the city. . . .

The ground plan of the city is shaped like a military cloak. The long sides, which are both bounded by water, are thirty *stades* across. The short sides are formed by the isthmuses, which are each seven or eight *stades* in breadth and are hemmed in by the sea on one side and the lake on the other. The whole city is cut up by streets suitable for the riding of horses and the driving of chariots. Two, which are especially broad—being more than a *plethron* wide—meet at right angles and bisect each other.

Alexandria has many fine public precincts and palaces, which occupy a fourth or even a third of the city's whole perimeter; for just as each of the kings added some adornment to its public monuments, so each added his own residence to those already existing so that, in the words of Homer, "one was on top of another." All the palaces are connected to each other and to the harbor, including those outside the harbor. The Museum forms one portion of the palaces. It has a walkway, an arcade with benches, and a large building in which is located the dining hall of the scholars who belong to the Museum. The faculty has both property in common and a priest, who is in charge of the Museum and was formerly appointed by the kings and is now by Caesar [Augustus]. Also part of the palace complex is the building called the Sema, which is a circular structure in which are the tombs of the kings and that of Alexander. Ptolemy, the son of Lagus, because of greed and the desire to seize control of Egypt, anticipated Perdikkas by stealing the body of Alexander when he was bringing it back from Babylon and was turning toward this country. . . . Having brought the body of Alexander to Egypt, Ptolemy buried it in Alexandria, where it now still lies, but not, however, in the same sarcophagus; for the present one is of glass, but Ptolemy buried it in one of gold.

From "Alexandria in the Age of Cleopatra." In D. Brendan Nagle and Stanley M. Burstein, *The Ancient World: Readings in Social and Cultural History* (Englewood Cliffs, NJ: Prentice Hall, 1995), pp. 154–55.

The river, [since it will not have] sufficient water, [will flood], but only a little so that scorched will be [the land   ] but unnaturally. [For] in the [time] of the Typhonians [people will say] "Wretched Egypt, [you have been] maltreated by the [terrible] malefactors who have committed evil against you." And the sun will darken as it will not be willing to observe the evils in Egypt. The earth will not respond to seeds. These will be part of its blight. [The] farmer will be dunned for taxes for what he did not plant. There will be fighting in Egypt because people will be in need of food. What one plants, [another] will slaughter which [will kill] brothers and wives. For [these things will happen] when the great god Hephaistos will desire to return to the [city], and the Girdlewearers (sc. Greeks) will kill each other as they [are Typhonians.   ] evil will be done. And he will pursue (them) on foot [to the] sea [in] wrath and destroy many of them because [they are] impious. The king will come from Syria, he who will be hateful to all men, [   ] . . . and from Aithiopia there will come . . . He (together with some) of the unholy ones (will come) to Egypt, and he will settle [in the city, which] later will be deserted. . . . Their children will be made weak, and the country will be in confusion, and many of the inhabitants of Egypt will abandon their homes and travel to foreign places. Then there will be slaughter among friends; and people will lament their own problems although they are less than those of others. Men will die at the hands of each other; two of them will come to the same place *to aid one*. Among women who are pregnant death will also be common. The Girdlewearers will kill themselves as they also are Typhonians. Then Agathos Daimon will abandon the city (sc. Alexandria) that had been founded and enter Memphis, and the city of foreigners, which had been founded, will be deserted. This will happen at the end of the evils of the time when there came to Egypt a crowd of foreigners. The city of the Girdlewearers will be abandoned like my kiln because of the crimes, which they committed against Egypt. The cult images, which had been transported there, will be brought back again to

Egypt; and the city by the sea will be a refuge for fishermen because Agathos Daimon and Knephis will have gone to Memphis, so that passersby will say "All-nurturing was this city in which every race of men settled." Then will Egypt flourish when the generous fifty-five year ruler appears, the king descended from Helios, the giver of good things, the one installed by the greatest, so that the living will pray that the dead might arise to share the prosperity. Finally the leaves will fall. The Nile, which had lacked water, will be full and winter, which had changed its orderly ways, will run its proper course and then summer will resume its own track, and normal will be the wind's breezes, which previously had been weak. For in the time of the Typhonians the sun will darken to highlight the character of the evils and to reveal the greed of the Girdlewearers. And Egypt [   ]. Having spoken clearly up to this point, he fell silent. King Amenophis, who was grieved by the many disasters he had recounted, buried the potter in Heliopolis and placed the book in the sacred archives there and unselfishly revealed it to all men. Speech of the potter to King Amenophis, <translated> as accurately as possible, concerning what will happen in Egypt.

From "A World without Greeks: The *Potter's Oracle.*" In Stanley M. Burstein, *The Hellenistic Age from the Battle of Ipsos to the Death of Kleopatra VII* (Cambridge: Cambridge University Press, 1985), pp. 136–137.

DOCUMENT 5
Ptolemaic Egypt: A Multicultural Society

The six documents in this section illustrate the complexity of social relations in Ptolemaic Egypt. The first three selections document the existence of tension between the native Egyptian population and privileged Greek and Jewish immigrants. It is a mistake, however, to see Ptolemaic Egypt as divided into mutually hostile ethnic groups. The Rosetta stone commemorates the coronation of Ptolemy V in 196 B.C.E. according to Egyptian rites, and highlights the mutual dependence of the Egyptian priesthood and the royal family. The fifth and sixth selections—the tomb biography of Pasherenptah III, high priest of Ptah, and an honorary decree for Kallimakhos, governor of the Thebaid—reveal the thoroughly multicultural character of the elite of Egypt in the time of Cleopatra VII.

. . . to Zenon, greeting. You do well if you keep your health. I too am well. You know that you left me in Syria with Krotos and I did every-thing that was ordered in respect to the camels and was blameless to-ward you. When you sent an order to give me pay, he gave nothing of what you ordered. When I asked repeatedly that he give me what you ordered and Krotos gave me nothing, but kept telling me to remove myself, I held out for a long time waiting for you; but when I was in want of necessities and could get nothing anywhere, I was compelled to run away into Syria so that I might not perish of hunger. So I wrote you that you might know that Krotos was the cause of it. When you sent me again to Philadelphia to Jason, although I do everything that is ordered, for nine months now he gives me nothing of what you or-dered me to have, neither oil nor grain, except at two month periods, when he pays the clothing (allowances). And I am in difficulty both summer and winter. And he orders me to accept ordinary wine for salary. Well, they have treated me with scorn because I am a "barbar-ian." I beg you therefore, if it seems good to you, to give them orders that I am to obtain what is owing and that in future they pay me in full, in order that I may not perish of hunger because I do not know how to act like a Greek. You, therefore, kindly cause a change in atti-tude toward me. I pray to all the gods and to the guardian divinity of the King that you remain and come to us so that you may yourself see that I am blameless. Farewell.

From "A Case of Discrimination." In *Business Papers of the Third Century* B.C. *Dealing with Palestine and Egypt*, vol. 2, ed. W. L. Westermann, C. W. Keyes, and H. Liebesny (New York: Columbia University Press, 1940), n. 66.

To Dionysios one of the friends and *strategos*, from Ptolemaios, son of Glaukias, Macedonian, of those in *katoche* in the great Serapeum in Memphis in my 12th year. Being outrageously wronged and often put in danger of my life by the below-listed cleaners from the sanctuary, I am seeking refuge with you thinking that I shall thus particularly receive jus-tice. For in the 21st year, on Phaophi 8, they came to the Astartieion in the sanctuary, in which I have been in *katoche* for the aforesaid years, some of them holding stones in their hands, others sticks, and tried to force their way in, so that with this opportunity they might plunder the temple and kill me because I am a Greek, attacking me in concerted fashion. And when I made it to the door of the temple before them and shut it with a great crash, and ordered them to go away quietly, they did not depart; but they struck Diphilos, one of the servants compelled to remain by Sarapis, who showed his indignation at the way they were behaving in the sanctuary, robbing him outrageously and attacking him violently and beating him, so that their illegal violence was made obvious to everybody. When the same men did the same things to me in Phaophi of the 19th year, I petitioned you at that time, but because I had no one to wait on you it happened that when they went unwarned they conceived an even greater scorn for me. I ask you, therefore, if it seems good to you, to order them brought before you, so that they may get the proper punishment for all these things. Farewell.

Mys the clothing seller, Psoisnaus the yoke-bearer, Imouthes the baker, Harembasnis the grain-seller, Stotoetis the porter, Harchebis the doucher, Po [   ] os the carpet weaver, and others with them, whose names I do not know.

From "Petition Concerning an Assault on a Greek (UPZ 18^{328})." In Roger S. Bagnall and Peter Derow, eds., *The Hellenistic Period: Historical Sources in Translation* (Oxford: Blackwell Publishing, 2004), pp. 232–33.

For he [Lysimachos] says that in the reign of Bocchoris, the king of Egypt, the Jewish people, who were lepers and had scabs and other illnesses, took refuge in the temples and asked for food. There were, however, very many people whose illnesses required care and there was a famine in Egypt. Bocchoris, the king of the Egyptians, sent to Ammon men to consult the oracle about the famine, and the god replied that he was to cleanse the temples of the unholy and impious men, driving them from the temples into the desert, to drown those with scabs and the lepers because the sun was angry at their life, and he was to consecrate the temples, and in this way the earth would become fruitful.

After receiving the oracle, Bocchoris summoned the priests and the sacrificers, and ordered them to select out the impure people and to hand them over to the soldiers, who would lead them into the desert, and would bind the lepers in lead sheets so they would sink into the sea. After the lepers and the people afflicted with scabs had been drowned, the rest who had been gathered together in desolate places were left to die. They, however, assembled and took thought for themselves, and when night came, they saved themselves by kindling fire and torches. On the next night they fasted and appealed to the gods to save them. The next day a certain Moses advised them to set out on a new course and follow a straight path until they came to places that were inhabited. He also advised them to display good will to no man nor to give good advice but always bad, and to destroy the temples and altars of the gods they might encounter.

After the rest of the people agreed, and they did what had been decided, traveling through the desert. After suffering considerably, they came to inhabited land; and after abusing the people and looting and burning the temples, they entered the country now called Judaea, and founded a city and settled down there. This city was called "Hierosyla" ("City of Temple-Robbers") from the character of the people. Later, however, when they had become powerful, they changed the name to one that was not offensive, and called the city Hierosolyma and themselves Hieroslymites.

From "An Antisemitic Account of the Exodus." In Josephos, *Against Apion* 1.304, trans. Stanley M. Burstein.

TITLES OF PTOLEMY V AS PHARAOH

In the reign of the young (god) who received the kingship from his father, Lord of crowns, great of fame, who established Egypt, and toward the gods is reverent, victorious over his enemies; who improved the life of men, lord of the thirty-year cycle as Hephaistos the Great, (and) king just as Helios; great king of the upper and lower lands, son of the gods Philopatores, whom Hephaistos approved, to whom Helios gave victory, living image of Zeus; son of Helios, Ptolemy, living forever, beloved of Ptah. Ninth year, in which Aetos, son of Aetos, is priest of Alexander and of the gods Soteres and of the gods Adelphoi and of the gods Euergetes and of the gods Philopatores and of the gods Epiphanes Eucharistos, and in which the athlophoros of Berenike Euergetes is Pyrrha, the daughter of Philon, the kanephoros of Arsinoe Philadelphos is Areia, the daughter of Diogenes, the priestess of Arsinoe Philopator is Eirene, the daughter of Ptolemy. Fourth day of the month Xandikos and the eighteenth day of the Egyptian month Mecheir.

DECREE

The high priest and prophets and those who enter the sanctuary for the robing of the gods, and the feather bearers and the sacred scribes and all the other priests, who, having come from the temples in the country to Memphis to be with the king for the celebration of the coronation of Ptolemy, living forever, beloved of Ptah, Epiphanes Eucharistos, successor of his father, and having met in the temple at Memphis on this day, introduced the following motion. King Ptolemy, living forever, beloved of Ptah, Epiphanes Eucharistos, son of King Ptolemy and Queen Arsinoe, Gods Philopatores, has conferred benefits in many ways on the temples and their staffs and on all those subject to his rule, as he is a god from a god and goddess just as Horos, the son of Isis and Osiris, the defender of his father Osiris; (and) being in matters concerning the gods benevolently inclined, he has assigned to the temples revenues in money and grain; and he has undertaken many expenses for the purpose of making Egypt prosperous and establishing the temples. With his own resources he has assisted everyone; and of the imposts and taxes in Egypt, some he has remitted entirely and others he has lightened in order that the people and everyone else may live in prosperity during his reign; and debts owed the crown by those in Egypt and the rest of his kingdom he has cancelled; and those being held in jails and those who had been detained because of accusations for a long time he has freed of charges. Likewise also he distributed justice to all just as Hermes the Great; and he gave orders that those of the *machimoi* who had returned together with the others who had been disaffected during the period of disturbances should remain in their own homes. He also provided that cavalry and infantry forces and ships be sent against those attacking Egypt by sea and land, undertaking great expenditures of money and provisions so that the temples and all in Egypt might be secure. And having arrived at Lykopolis in the Bousirite (nome), which had been seized and had been readied for a siege with an abundant store of weapons and all other provisions since the conspiracy had been prepared over a long period of time by impious men who had gathered together in it and who had committed many evil (acts) against the temples and the inhabitants of Egypt, he encamped opposite it and surrounded the city with mounds and ditches and wondrous walls. As the Nile flood in the eighth year was great and normally covered the plains, he restrained it by blocking in many places the mouths of the canals, having spent not a little money on these things; and, having stationed cavalry and infantry to guard them, in a short time he took the city by force and destroyed all the impious men in it, as Hermes and Horos, the son of Isis and Osiris, dealt with the rebels in these same places formerly. Those who had led the rebels in the time of his own father and caused [disorder] in the land and desecrated the temples, when he arrived at Memphis to avenge his father and his realm, he punished all of them fittingly at the time he arrived to perform the rites connected with his coronation.

(Since these things are so), with good fortune, it has been resolved by the priests of all the temples in the land that [all] honors belonging to King Ptolemy, the eternal, beloved of Ptah, god Epiphanes Eucharistos, and likewise also those of his parents, the gods Philopatores, and those of his grandparents, the gods Euergetes, [and those] of the gods Philadelphoi and those of the gods Soteres, shall be increased greatly; and they shall set up a statue of King Ptolemy, the eternal, god Epiphanes Eucharistos, in each temple in the most prominent [place], which shall be called (the image of) Ptolemy the Avenger of Egypt, and beside which shall stand the chief god of the temple, and there shall be given to it a weapon of victory prepared [in Egyptian] style, and the priests shall perform cult service to these images three times a day and dress them in sacred apparel and perform all the other ritual acts just as (is done) for the other gods in [the native] festivals.

From "The King and the Temples: The Rosetta Stone." In Stanley M. Burstein, *The Hellenistic Age from the Battle of Ipsos to the Death of Kleopatra VII* (Cambridge: Cambridge University Press, 1985), pp. 130–31.

In the year 25, on the 21st of Phaophi, in the reign of the king, the lord of the land, Ptolemy, the Savior God, the Conqueror, was the day whereon I was born. I lived thirteen years in the presence of my father. There went forth a command from the king, the lord of the land, the Father-loving Sister-loving God, the New Osiris, son of the Sun, Lord of Diadems, Ptolemy, that the high office of High Priest of Memphis should be conferred upon me, I being then fourteen years old. I set the adornment of the serpent-crown upon the head of the king on the day that he took possession of Upper Egypt and Lower Egypt, and performed all the customary rites in the chambers, which are appointed for the Thirty

Years' Festivals. I was leader in all the secret offices. I gave instruction for the consecration of the Horus [the king as divine] at the time of the birth of the [Sun-]god [i.e., the spring equinox] in the Golden House. I betook me to the residence of the kings of the Ionians [the Greek kings], which is on the shore of the Great Sea to the west of Rakoti. The king of Upper and Lower Egypt, the Master of two worlds, the Father-loving Sister-loving God, the New Osiris, was crowned in his royal palace. He proceeded to the temple of Isis, the Lady of Yat-udjat. He offered unto her sacrifices many and costly. Riding in his chariot forth from the temple of Isis, the king himself caused his chariot to stand still. He wreathed my head with a beautiful wreath of gold and all manner of gems, except only the royal pectoral, which was on his own breast. I was nominated Prophet, and he sent out a royal rescript to the capitals of all the nomes, saying:

"I have appointed the High Priest of Memphis, Pasherenptah (III), to be my Prophet." And there was delivered to me from the temples of Upper Egypt and Lower Egypt a yearly revenue for my maintenance.

The king came to Memphis on a feast-day. He passed up and down in his ship that he might behold both sides of the place. So soon as he landed at the quarter of the city called Onkhtawy, he went into the temple escorted by his magnates and his wives and his royal children, with all the things prepared for the feast; sitting in the ship, he sailed up, in order to celebrate the feast in honor of all the gods who dwell in Memphis, according to the greatness of the goodwill in the heart of the lord of the land, and the white crown was upon his brow.

I was a great man, rich in all riches, whereby I possessed a goodly harem. I lived forty-three years without any man-child being born to me. In which matter the majesty of this glorious god, Imhotep, the son of Ptah, was gracious unto me. A man-child was bestowed upon me, who was called Imhotep, and was surnamed Petubast. Tayimhotep, the daughter of the father of the god, the Prophet of Horus, the lord of Letopolis, Kha-hapi, was his mother.

Under the majesty of the princess, the lady of the land, Kleopatra and of her son Kaisar in the year 11, the 15th of Phamenoth was the day on which I was carried into the haven. I was brought to the necropolis, and there was performed upon me every rite customary for a well-prepared mummy. The laying in the grave took place in the year 12 on the 30th of Thoth. The years of my life in all were forty and nine.

From "Biographical Inscription of Pasherenptah III, High Priest of Ptah during the Reigns of Ptolemy XII and Cleopatra VII." Adapted from the translation of S.R.K. Glanville published in E. Bevan, *The House of Ptolemy: A History of Egypt under the Ptolemaic Dynasty* (London: Arnold, 1927), pp. 347–48.

[In the reign of Cleop]atra (VII), goddess [Ph]ilopat[or and of P]tolemaios, who is also the son of Kaisar, god Philopator, god Philometor, [year 13, Art]emisios 18, Phamenoth 18. It has been resolved by the priests from Diospolis the Great, (priests) of the [greatest god, Amo]nrasonther, both the elders and all the others. Kallimakhos, the kinsman, [and *strategos* and] revenue officer for the district of Thebes, and gymnasiarch and cavalry-commander, previously having taken over the city, which had been ruined [as a result of manifold [disastrous] circumstances, tended it carefully and maintained it] unburdened [in] complete peace. Moreover, he reverently outfitted the sanctuaries of the great ancestral gods, and the lives [of those in them he saved]; and, in general, he made a [   ]. In addition, he restored everything [to its former] prosperous state and strengthened truth and justice. And, indeed, [he displayed] his goodness of heart, and in beneficence those who excel in generosity. And further, now . . . [the] severe famine caused by a crop-failure like none hitherto recorded, and when the city had been almost crushed by [need], he, having devoted himself wholeheartedly, voluntarily contributed to the salvation of each of the local inhabitants. Having labored [as a father on behalf] of his own fatherland and his legitimate children, with the good will of the gods, in continuous abundance of [food] he maintained nearly everyone; and [he kept them] unaware of the circumstance from which he furnished the abundance. The famine, however, continued in the present year and became even worse and [   ] a failure of the flood and misery far worse than ever before reigning throughout the *whole* [land] and the condition of the city being wholly critical . . . and all having become weak from want and virtually everyone seeking everything, but [no one] obtaining it, he, having called upon the greatest god, who then stood at his side, [Amonrasonth]er, and having nobly shouldered by himself the burden again, just as a bright star and a good daimon, he shone upon [everyone]. For he dedicated his life wholly . . . for the inhabitants of the district of Thebes, and, having nourished and saved everyone together with their wives and children, just as from [a gale and] contending winds, he brought them into a safe harbor. But the chief and greatest (indication) [of his piety] (was the fact that), being in charge of everything connected with the divine, to the greatest degree possible he reverently and sleeplessly took thought [for the sacred rites] so that from the time his grandfather, Kallimakhos, the kinsman and epistrategos, [renewed them], the processions of the lord gods and the festivals have been held in a most holy and excellent manner just as in [ancient times]. (Since these things are so), with good fortune, he shall be addressed as savior of the city, which is ancient [   ] on his birthday in important places in the sanctuary of the great god, Amonrasonther; [three statues of him, one] of hard stone the priests and two, one of bronze and the other likewise of hard stone, the city (shall set up); [and every year they shall celebrate] this same day as his nameday and offer sacrifice to the lord gods and wear wreaths and hold a feast, [just as is customary]; and they shall inscribe the decree on a stone stele in both Greek and native letters [and set it up on] the floor of the temple so that publicly he shall share in the [goodwill] of the greatest god, [Amonrasonther], in order that for all time his benefactions shall exist in everlasting memory.

From "Honorary Decree for Kallimakhos, Governor of Thebes, March 39." In Stanley M. Burstein, *The Hellenistic Age from the Battle of Ipsos to the Death of Kleopatra VII* (Cambridge: Cambridge University Press, 1985), pp. 144–45.

DOCUMENT 6
Religion in Ptolemaic Egypt

In the multicultural society of Ptolemaic Egypt, one of the areas in which Greeks and Egyptians met was religion. The two documents in this section illustrate this interaction. The first tells how the cult statue of Sarapis, the patron deity of Alexandria, was discovered and brought to Egypt. Although the statue was made by the Greek sculptor Bryaxis in the form of a Greek god, Manetho and Timotheos of Athens used an old Egyptian literary form—the communication of the god's will directly to Ptolemy I in a dream—to authenticate the statue. In the second selection, the ancient Egyptian goddess Isis is reinterpreted as a mother goddess and founder of civilization through identification with various Greek goddesses.

The origin of this God Serapis has not hitherto been made generally known by our writers. The Egyptian priests give this account. While

Ptolemy, the first Macedonian king who consolidated the power of Egypt, was setting up in the newly built city of Alexandria fortifications, temples, and rites of worship, there appeared to him in his sleep a youth of singular beauty and more than human stature, who counseled the monarch to send his most trusty friends to Pontus, and fetch his effigy from that country. This, he said, would bring prosperity to the realm, and great and illustrious would be the city which gave it a reception. At the same moment he saw the youth ascend to heaven in a blaze of fire. Roused by so significant and strange an appearance, Ptolemy disclosed the vision of the night to the Egyptian priests, whose business it is to understand such matters. As they knew but little of Pontus or of foreign countries, he enquired of Timotheus, an Athenian, one of the family of the Eumolpids, whom he had invited from Eleusis to preside over the sacred rites, what this worship was, and who was the deity. Timotheus, questioning persons who had found their way to Pontus, learnt that there was there a city Sinope, and near it a temple, which, according to an old tradition of the neighborhood, was sacred to the infernal Jupiter, for there also stood close at hand a female figure, to which many gave the name of Proserpine. Ptolemy, however, with the true disposition of a despot, though prone to alarm, was, when the feeling of security returned, more intent on pleasures than on religious matters; and he began by degrees to neglect the affair, and to turn his thoughts to other concerns, till at length the same apparition, but now more terrible and peremptory, denounced ruin against the king and his realm, unless his bidding were performed. Ptolemy then gave directions that an embassy should be dispatched with presents to king Scydrothemis, who at that time ruled the people of Sinope, and instructed them, when they were on the point of sailing, to consult the Pythian Apollo. Their voyage was prosperous, and the response of the oracle was clear. The God bade them go and carry back with them the image of his father, but leave that of his sister behind.

On their arrival at Sinope, they delivered to Scydrothemis the presents from their king, with his request and message. He wavered in purpose, dreading at one moment the anger of the God, terrified at another by the threats and opposition of the people. Often he was wrought upon by the gifts and promises of the ambassadors. And so three years passed away, while Ptolemy did not cease to urge his zealous solicitations. He continued to increase the dignity of his embassies, the number of his

ships, and the weight of his gold. A terrible vision then appeared to Scydrothemis, warning him to thwart no longer the purposes of the God. As
he yet hesitated, various disasters, pestilence, and the unmistakable anger
of heaven, which grew heavier from day to day, continued to harass him.
He summoned an assembly, and explained to them the bidding of the
God, the visions of Ptolemy and himself, and the miseries that were gathering about them. The people turned away angrily from their king, were
jealous of Egypt, and, fearing for themselves, thronged around the temple. The story becomes at this point more marvelous, and relates that the
God of his own will conveyed himself on board the fleet, which had been
brought close to shore, and, wonderful to say, vast as was the extent of
sea that they traversed, they arrived at Alexandria on the third day. A
temple, proportioned to the grandeur of the city, was erected in a place
called Rhacotis, where there had stood a chapel consecrated in old times
to Serapis and Isis. Such is the most popular account of the origin and
introduction of the God Serapis. I am aware indeed that there are some
who say that he was brought from Seleucia, a city of Syria, in the reign
of Ptolemy III, while others assert that it was the act of the same king,
but that the place from which he was brought was Memphis, once a famous city and the strength of ancient Egypt. The God himself, because
he heals the sick, many identified him with Aesculapius; others with
Osiris, the deity of the highest antiquity among these nations; not a few
with Jupiter, as being supreme ruler of all things; but most people with
Pluto, arguing from the emblems which may be seen on his statues, or
from conjectures of their own.

From Tacitus, "The Origin of Sarapis," *Histories*, 4.83–84. In *The Complete Works
of Tacitus*, trans. John Church and William Jackson Brodribb (New York: Ran-
dom House, 1942), pp. 653–55.

Demetrios, the son of Artemidoros, who is also called Thraseas, a Mag-
nesian from Magnesia on the Maeander, an offering in fulfillment of a
vow to Isis. He transcribed the following from the stele in Memphis
which stands by the temple of Hephaistos:

> I am Isis, the tyrant of every land; and I was educated by Hermes,
> and together with Hermes I invented letters, both the hieroglyphic
> and the demotic, in order that the same script should not be used

to write everything. I imposed laws on men, and the laws which I laid down no one may change. I am the eldest daughter of Kronos. I am the wife and sister of King Osiris. I am she who discovered the cultivation of grain for men. I am the mother of King Horos. I am she who rises in the Dog Star. I am she who is called goddess by women. By me the city of Bubastis was built. I separated earth from sky. I designated the paths of the stars. The sun and the moon's course I laid out. I invented navigation. I caused the just to be strong. Woman and man I brought together. For woman I determined that in the tenth month she shall deliver a baby into the light. I ordained that parents be cherished by their children. For parents who are cruelly treated I imposed retribution. Together with my brother Osiris I stopped cannibalism. I revealed initiations to men. I taught men to honor the images of the gods. I established precincts for the gods. The governments of tyrants I suppressed. I stopped murders. I compelled women to be loved by men. I caused the just to be stronger than gold and silver. I ordained that the true be considered beautiful. I invented marriage contracts. Languages I assigned to Greeks and barbarians. I caused the honorable and the shameful to be distinguished by Nature. I caused nothing to be more fearful than an oath. He who unjustly plotted against others I gave into the hands of his victim. On those who commit unjust acts I imposed retribution. I ordained that suppliants be pitied. I honor those who justly defend themselves. With me the just prevails. Of rivers and winds and the sea am I mistress. No one becomes famous without my knowledge. I am the mistress of war. Of the thunderbolt am I mistress. I calm and stir up the sea. I am in the rays of the sun. I sit beside the course of the sun. Whatever I decide, this also is accomplished. For me everything is right. I free those who are in bonds. I am the mistress of sailing. The navigable I make unnavigable whenever I choose. I established the boundaries of cities. I am she who is called Lawgiver. The island from the depths I brought up into the light. I conquer Fate. Fate heeds me. Hail Egypt who reared me.

From "The Praises of Isis, Mistress of the Universe and Creator of Civilization." In Stanley M. Burstein, *The Hellenistic Age from the Battle of Ipsos to the Death of Kleopatra VII* (Cambridge: Cambridge University Press, 1985), p. 147.

APPENDIX: THE PTOLEMIES

GLOSSARY OF SELECTED TERMS

Agathos Daimon: The "good daimon"; the patron god of Alexandria, who was identified with Shay, the Egyptian god of Fate.

Amenophis: Greek name for the eighteenth dynasty Egyptian king Amenhotep III, who reigned from 1390 to 1352 B.C.E.

Amonrasonther: Greek rendering of Amon-Re, king of the gods, the chief god of Thebes.

Amphora: A large thick-walled ceramic storage jar, usually with a sharply tapering base. Used to store or transport liquid or dry staples such as wine, olive oil, and grain.

Aroura: In Egypt, a measure of land equal to about ⅔ of an acre.

Artaba: An Egyptian grain measure equal to about 40 choinikes—i.e., scoopfuls—or about 39 quarts.

Artemisios: Seventh month of the Macedonian calendar, equivalent to March. In the late Ptolemaic period, the Macedonian and Egyptian calendars were synchronized, so they both began in October.

Athlophoros: "Prize-bearer"; title of the deified Berenike II, the wife of Ptolemy III.

Bocchoris: Greek name for the Egyptian king Bakenrenef, the sole king of the twenty-fourth dynasty. He reigned from 720 to 715 B.C.E.

Choinix: An Egyptian grain measure equal to approximately ¼₀ of a quart.

Chrematistai: A three-judge panel that formed an itinerant court open to Greeks and Egyptians. They judged cases in which issues were framed in Greek.

Cleruchy: A cleruch was an immigrant soldier, who received as part of his pay a conditional grant of land called a cleruchy. Originally cleruchies were held for as long as the soldiers performed military service and then returned to the government for reassignment. By Cleopatra's time, however, they had become hereditary and were treated as essentially the property of the cleruch and his family.

Dekanos: Title of an officer in charge of a group of ten men. It could be used as a general title as well as for the heads of groups of ten employed in various functions, such as police.

Dioiketes: Chief financial officer and head of the administration.

Dionysos: Greek god of wine and intoxication identified with the Egyptian god Osiris. Also within his sphere were the theater and related activities, ritual ecstasy, and the afterlife.

Diospolis the Great: "The great city of Zeus"; Greek name for the Egyptian city of Thebes. Its name derived from the identification of Amon, the chief god of Thebes, with Zeus.

Drachma: A standard of weight as well as a coin. There were six obols to a drachma, sixty drachmas to a mina, and sixty minas to a talent. The weight and value of a drachma varied widely in the Hellenistic period.

Ephebe: A year of mandatory service for Greek boys in their late teens that marked their transition to adult-citizen status. At Alexandria, the ephebate was primarily devoted to education and connected to membership in the gymnasia. Completion of the ephebate was required of all Alexandrian citizens.

Epiphanes: "Manifest"; royal cult title that refers to the manifestation in the person of the king of either divine traits or a new divinity.

Epistrategos: Originally a high-level military officer. In the late Ptolemaic period, it was the title of the governor of the Thebaid—the seven southernmost nomes of Upper Egypt—and one of the highest-ranking officials in Egypt.

Eucharistos: "Gracious"; cult title of Ptolemy V.

Euergetes: Royal cult epithet meaning "benefactor" that was borne by Ptolemy III and Ptolemy VIII.

Girdlewearers: Greeks and Macedonians.

Hasmoneans: Jewish priestly and royal family that traced its origin to Matthias, who began the rebellion against Seleukid rule in Judaea in 167 B.C.E. Ruled Judaea until 63 B.C.E. and continued to be prominent in Jewish affairs until the early 30s B.C.E.

Kanephoros: "Basket bearer"; title of the priestess of the deified Arsinoe II.

Katoche: "Detention"; Katoche refers to the situation of individuals who believed that they were required to live within the precincts of the Temple of Sarapis at Memphis by order of the god.

Kinsman: Title of honor borne by Ptolemaic officials. It was the highest rank at the Ptolemaic court.

Komarch: Village headman. The komarch was in charge of the civil administration of a village.

Laokritai: Egyptian judges who administered Egyptian law in Egyptian.

Machimoi: Members of the native Egyptian military caste.

Mecheir: Sixth month of the Egyptian calendar, equivalent to February in the late Ptolemaic period.

Mesore: Twelfth month of the Egyptian calendar, equivalent to June–July in the Ptolemaic period.

Mnevis: A sacred bull like Apis and Buchis. Mnevis was believed to be the son and representative on earth of the sun god Re of Heliopolis (city of the sun) in the northeastern Delta.

Nomarch: Administrative official in charge of the agricultural production of a nome.

Nome: One of the administrative districts that formed the basis of the organization of Egypt in the pharaonic and Ptolemaic periods. In the pharaonic period, there were usually forty-two nomes. In the Ptolemaic period, the number of nomes varied from thirty-six to forty.

Pachon: Ninth month of the Egyptian calendar, equivalent to May in the late Ptolemaic period.

Paralogeia: Additional taxes collected without official authorization.

Phamenoth: Seventh month of the Egyptian calendar, equivalent to March in the late Ptolemaic period.

Phaophi: Second month of the Egyptian calendar, equivalent to October in the late Ptolemaic period.

Pharmouthi: Eighth month of the Egyptian calendar, equivalent to April in the late Ptolemaic period.

Philometor: "Mother loving god"; royal cult title of Ptolemy VI.

Philopator: "Father loving god"; royal cult title of Ptolemy IV, Ptolemy XII, and Cleopatra VII.

Polis: "City"; in Greece, the polis was the principal form of socio-political organization. A polis was a self-governing civic community and consisted of a central city or town and its surrounding rural territory. There were only three poleis in Egypt: Alexandria, Naukratis, and Ptolemais.

Ptah: Ancient creator god of Memphis. Ptah's primary association was with craftsmen, and he was identified for that reason with the Greek god Hephaistos.

Satrapy: Term for one of the twenty provinces into which the Persian Empire was divided. Governors were called satraps. The system was retained by Alexander the Great and his successors.

Sitologoi: Managers of royal granaries in a nome.

Stade: A Greek measure of distance. There were eight stades in a mile.

Strategos: "General"; in Ptolemaic Egypt, *strategoi* replaced nomarchs as the governors of nomes.

Talent: A Greek weight or amount of money. A talent was equal to six thousand drachmas or sixty minas. The weight of a talent varied from 57 pounds to 83 pounds depending on the standard used.

Thebaid: A subdivision of Upper Egypt consisting of the seven southernmost nomes from Thebes to the First Cataract at Syene, modern Aswan.

Thoth: Egyptian god of writing and knowledge. In the Ptolemaic period, Thoth was usually identified with the Greek god Hermes.

Thyrsos: A staff topped with a pine cone and decorated with fillets that was used by celebrants in the cult of the Greek god Dionysos.

Toga virilis: A man's toga, which a Roman boy assumed at his coming of age ceremony on his seventeenth birthday.

Toparchy: Administrative subdivision; a nome consisted of several villages. Its administrator was a toparch.

Typhonians: The followers of the Greek mythical monster Typhon, who was identified with Seth—the brother and enemy of Osiris and god of the desert, foreigners, and evil.

NOTES

PREFACE

1. The most comprehensive treatment of the historiography of Ptolemaic Egypt is Alan E. Samuel, *The Shifting Sands of History: Interpretations of Ptolemaic Egypt* (Lanham, MD: University of Press of America, 1989). For a brief overview of subsequent developments, see Stanley M. Burstein, "The Hellenistic Age," in Stanley M. Burstein et al., *Ancient History: Recent Work and New Directions* (Claremont: Regina Books, 1997), pp. 50–52.

CLEOPATRA'S LIFE

1. For the details of the case, see the work of the German historian Werner Huss, "Die Herkunft des Cleopatra Philopator," *Aegyptus* 70 (1990): 191–203. The core of the argument is threefold: (1) Strabo's evidence that Cleopatra was illegitimate—that is, that her mother was neither a Macedonian nor a Greek; (2) only "marriage" with an Egyptian family of the highest rank such as that of the high priests of Ptah would be suitable; and (3) marriage connections between the Ptolemies and this family are already attested in the late second century B.C.E.

2. H. W. Fairman, ed., "The Hieroglyphic Inscriptions," in Sir Robert Mond and Oliver H. Myers, *The Bucheum*, vol. 2, *The Inscriptions* (London: The Egypt Exploration Society, 1934), n. 13.

3. *Alexandrian War*, p. 33.

4. For the chronology of Cleopatra's visits to Rome, I follow the reconstruction of Erich Gruen, "Cleopatra in Rome: Facts and Fantasies," in *Myth, History, and Culture in Republican Rome*, ed. D. Braund and C. Gill (Exeter, 2003), pp. 257–74.

5. The Jewish author of the third book of the Sybilline Oracles, writing probably before the Battle of Actium, predicts that a widowed queen of Egypt, who can only be Cleopatra VII, will destroy Rome, *The Sibylline Oracles*, book 3, lines

46–93, in *The Old Testament Pseudepigrapha*, ed. James H. Charles Worth, vol. 1 (Garden City: Doubleday, 1983), pp. 363–64.

PTOLEMAIC EGYPT: HOW DID IT WORK?

1. P. Van Minnen, "An Official Act of Cleopatra," *Ancient Society* 30 (2000): 32.

2. The story is conveniently told in Naphtali Lewis, *Greeks in Ptolemaic Egypt* (Oxford: Oxford University Press, 1986), pp. 104–5.

3. Appian, *Roman History*, preface, p. 10.

CLEOPATRA'S EGYPT: A MULTICULTURAL SOCIETY

1. Theokritos, *Idyll* 14, line 58.

2. Theokritos, *Idyll* 15, lines 47–48.

3. Gideon Bohak, "CPJ III 520: The Egyptian Reaction to Onias' Temple," *Journal for the Study of Judaism* 26 (1995): 34.

4. *The Prophecy of the Lamb* is translated in William K. Simpson, R. O. Faulkner, E. F. Wente Jr., and Robert Ritner, eds., *The Literature of Ancient Egypt*, 3rd ed. (New Haven: Yale University Press, 2003), pp. 445–49.

5. "Greek status" raised Jews above Egyptians, but it did not make them citizens of Alexandria and the other two Greek cities as can be seen from the fact that Cleopatra excluded them from an emergency distribution of grain during a famine (Josephos, *Against Apion* 2.56) in accordance with the traditional Greek principle that only citizens had the right to a share of the city's resources.

ALEXANDRIA: CITY OF CULTURE AND CONFLICT

1. It was supposed to be a fortress that defended Egypt by means of a huge mirror that detected enemy ships while they were still at sea, *Chau Ju-Kua: His Work on the Chinese and Arab Trade in the Twelfth and Thirteenth Centuries, entitled Chu-fan-chi*, trans. Friedrich Hirth and W. W. Rockhill (St. Petersburg, 1911), p. 146.

2. Polybius, Histories, 15.33.10.

CONCLUSION: QUEEN AND SYMBOL

1. Livy, *Roman History* 38.17.

2. Cassius Dio, *Roman History* 51.16.5.

3. Propertius, *Elegies* 3, ed. and trans. G. P. Goold (Cambridge, MA: Harvard University Press, 1990), lines 39–42 and 47–49.

4. Cassius Dio, *Roman History* 51.19.4.

5. Anonymous, *Liber de Viris Illustribus* 86. This brief entry is the only biography of Cleopatra to survive from antiquity.

6. Grace Harriet Macurdy, *Hellenistic Queens: A Study of Woman-Power in Macedonia, Seleucid Syria,* and *Ptolemaic Egypt* (Baltimore: Johns Hopkins University Press, 1932), p. 185.

7. The African American case for Cleopatra's being black was first made in J. A. Rogers, *World's Great Men of Color,* vol. 1 (New York: Collier Books, 1946), 129–30.

8. The use of Cleopatra in contemporary African American popular culture is discussed by Shelley P. Haley, "Black Feminist Thought and Classics: Remembering, Re-claiming, Re-empowering," in *Feminist Theory and the Classics,* ed. Nancy Sorkin Rabinowitz and Amy Richlin (New York: Routledge, 1993), pp. 28–31; and Fancesca T. Royster, *Becoming Cleopatra: The Shifting Image of an Icon* (New York: Palgrave Macmillan, 2003).

9. The fullest discussion is in Mary Lefkowitz, *Not Out of Africa: How Afrocentrism Became an Excuse to Teach Myth as History,* 2nd ed. (New York: Basic Books, 1997), pp. 34–52.

10. It is stated as a fact in the most recently published history of Ptolemaic Egypt in English. Gunther Hölbl, *A History of the Ptolemaic Empire,* trans. Tina Saavedra (London: Routledge, 2001), p. 223.

11. Haley, 28.

ANNOTATED BIBLIOGRAPHY

Books

Alexandria and Alexandrianism. Malibu: J. Paul Getty Museum, 1996. An extensively illustrated collection of essays dealing with the culture and legacy of Alexandria.

Agatharchides of Cnidus. *On the Erythraean Sea*. Edited and translated by Stanley M. Burstein. London: Hakluyt Society, 1989. A fully annotated translation of the principal source for Ptolemaic exploration and activity in Nubia and the Red Sea basin.

Arnold, Dieter. *Temples of the Last Pharaohs*. Oxford: Oxford University Press, 1999. A detailed survey and analysis of temple building in Egypt during the first millennium B.C.E. The work is particularly valuable for its discussion of temples built by the Ptolemies and their immediate predecessors but no longer extant.

Ashton, Sally-Ann. *The Last Queens of Egypt*. London: Pearson Education, Ltd., 2003. A lucid study of the representation of late Ptolemaic queens in contemporary Greek and Egyptian art.

Bagnall, Roger S. *Reading Papyri, Writing Ancient History*. London: Routledge, 1995. A brief introduction to the use of papyrological evidence for analyzing the social and economic history of Greco-Roman history.

Bagnall, Roger S., and Peter Derow, eds. *The Hellenistic Age: Historical Sources in Translation*. Oxford: Blackwell Publishing, 2004. An extensive sourcebook containing numerous papyrological texts illustrating the administrative and social history of Ptolemaic Egypt.

Bell, Idris H. *Cults and Creeds in Graeco-Roman Egypt*. Liverpool: Liverpool University Press, 1957. Four essays treating Greek, Egyptian, and Jewish religious interaction as illuminated by papyri and its significance for the development of Christianity in Egypt.

Bevan, Edwyn. *The House of Ptolemy: A History of Egypt under the Ptolemaic Dynasty*. London: Arnold, 1927. An old but still valuable history of Ptolemaic Egypt. Although strong on political and military history, the work is weak on social history and the Egyptian context of Ptolemaic history.

Bilde, Per, et al., eds. *Ethnicity in Hellenistic Egypt*. Aarhus: Aarhus University Press, 1992. A valuable collection of essays by European scholars on the varied responses of Greeks, Jews, and Egyptians to the development of a multicultural society in Ptolemaic Egypt.

Blum, Rudolf. *Kallimachos: The Alexandrian Library and the Origins of Bibliography*. Translated by Hans H. Wellisch. Madison: University of Wisconsin Press, 1991. A detailed technical study of Kallimachos' bibliographical work and its significance for the development of literary scholarship at the Alexandrian library.

Bowman, Alan K. *Egypt after the Pharaohs: 332 BC–AD 642: From Alexander to the Arab Conquest*. Berkeley and Los Angeles: University of California Press, 1986. A social and cultural history of Egypt from Alexander to the Arab conquest based on papyrological evidence.

Burstein, Stanley M. *The Hellenistic Age from the Battle of Ipsos to the Death of Kleopatra VII*. Cambridge: Cambridge University Press, 1985. A general sourcebook for Hellenistic history emphasizing epigraphical texts.

Canfora, Luciano. *The Vanished Library: A Wonder of the Ancient World*. Translated by Martin Ryle. London: Hutchinson Radius, 1989. An imaginative reconstruction of the history of the Alexandrian library with a valuable discussion of the literary sources for the library and its contents.

Casson, Lionel. *Libraries in the Ancient World*. New Haven: Yale University Press, 2001. A comprehensive history of ancient libraries, particularly valuable for its treatment of the archaeological evidence.

Chauveau, Michel. *Cleopatra: Beyond the Myth*. Translated by David Lorton. Ithaca: Cornell University Press, 2002. A revisionist study of Cleopatra by a leading French Egyptologist aiming to consider the evidence of the sources independent of the popular tradition concerning the queen as a sexual predator.

———. *Egypt in the Age of Cleopatra: History and Society under the Ptolemies*. Translated by David Lorton. Ithaca: Cornell University Press, 1997. A brief but valuable survey of the society and culture of Ptolemaic Egypt emphasizing the Egyptian evidence.

————. *Cleopatra's Egypt: Age of the Ptolemies*. Brooklyn: The Brooklyn Museum, 1988. The catalogue of the first major exhibit of the art of Egypt in the age of Cleopatra. It contains an important series of essays on the religious and artistic history of the period.

Crawford, Dorothy J. *Kerkeosiris: An Egyptian Village in the Ptolemaic Period*. Cambridge: Cambridge University Press, 1971. A vivid and detailed reconstruction of life in an Egyptian village based on papyrological evidence.

Empereur, Jean-Yves. *Alexandria Rediscovered*. New York: George Braziler Publisher, 1998. An extensively illustrated survey of recent archaeological discoveries in Alexandria, with particular emphasis on the results of the underwater excavations in Alexandria harbor.

Fraser, P. M. *Ptolemaic Alexandria*. Oxford: Oxford University Press. A massive survey of all that is known about the social and cultural history Ptolemaic Alexandria, marred only by its lack of any systematic treatment of the Egyptian aspects of the city's life. The second volume contains a comprehensive account of the classical evidence for the history of the city.

Gaddio, Franck, et al. *Alexandria: The Submerged Royal Quarters*. London: Periplus, 1998. A lavishly illustrated scholarly publication and analysis of the historical significance of underwater archaeological discoveries in Alexandria harbor.

Goudriaan, Koen. *Ethnicity in Ptolemaic Egypt*. Amsterdam: J. C. Gieben, 1988. A detailed collection and analysis of the evidence concerning ethnic identification in Ptolemaic Egypt that concludes that no single definition of "Greek" is possible.

Grant, Michael. *Cleopatra*. London: Weidenfeld and Nicolson, Ltd., 1972. Thoroughly documented biography by a prominent Roman historian. Successfully integrates Cleopatra's life into the history of the Roman civil wars without treating her reign as merely an episode in Roman history.

Green, Peter. *Alexander to Actium: The Historical Evolution of the Hellenistic Age*. Berkeley and Los Angeles: University of California Press, 1990. The standard comprehensive history of the Hellenistic period in English.

Hallett, Lucy Hughes. *Cleopatra: Histories, Dreams and Distortions*. New York: Harper and Row, 1990. Pioneering study of the treatment of Cleopatra in

Western culture. The discussion of Cleopatra in nineteenth- and twentieth-century popular culture is particularly good.

Hammer, Mary. *Signs of Cleopatra: History, Politics, Representation*. London: Routledge, 1993. Like Hallett, Hammer surveys the treatment of Cleopatra in Western culture from antiquity to the present, but with particular emphasis on her representation in European painting.

Hölbl, Gunther. *A History of the Ptolemaic Empire*. Translated by Tina Saavedra. London: Routledge, 2001. Standard contemporary history of Ptolemaic Egypt. Particularly notable is the extensive use of native Egyptian sources.

Huzar, Eleanor Goltz. *Mark Antony: A Biography*. Beckenham: Croom Helm, 1978. The standard biography of Mark Antony. Particularly useful for its full treatment of Antony's career before his involvement with Cleopatra.

Irby-Massie, Georgia L., and Paul T Keyser. *Greek Science of the Hellenistic Period: A Sourcebook*. London: Routledge, 2002. Valuable collection of primary sources dealing with the full range of Hellenistic science. Detailed introductions and headnotes put the translated texts into their historical context.

Jones, Prudence J. *Cleopatra: A Sourcebook*. University of Oklahoma Press, 2006. Well-edited collection of primary sources concerning Cleopatra's reign and her treatment in literature from the middle ages to the present.

Kleiner, Diana E. E. *Cleopatra and Rome*. Harvard University Press, 2005. Lucid, well-illustrated analysis of the significance of images of Cleopatra in the formation of Roman imperial culture.

Lewis, Naphtali. *Greeks in Ptolemaic Egypt: Case Studies in the Social History of the Hellenistic World*. Oxford: Oxford University Press, 1986. Chronologically arranged biographical sketches based on papyrological evidence of eight typical immigrant Greeks. The book provides an illuminating insight into the range of social and economic roles available to immigrants and their descendants in Ptolemaic Egypt.

————. *Papyrus in Classical Antiquity*. London: Oxford University Press, 1974. Valuable account of the preparation and use of papyrus. The book provides a case study of how one of the most important monopolies in Ptolemaic Egypt functioned.

Macurdy, Grace Harriet. *Hellenistic Queens: A Study of Woman-Power in Macedonia, Seleucid Syria, and Ptolemaic Egypt*. Baltimore: Johns Hopkins University Press, 1932. A pioneering study by a feminist historian of the role of queens in the Hellenistic period, with particular emphasis on their political influence.

Meier, Christian. *Caesar: A Biography.* New York: Basic Books, 1982. A detailed biography of Julius Caesar by a leading historian of the Roman republic.

Modrzejewski, Joseph Mélèze. *The Jews of Egypt: From Ramses II to Emperor Hadrian.* Translated by Robert Cornman. Philadelphia: Jewish Publication Society, 1995. Detailed study of the position of Jews in Egypt from the late second millennium B.C.E. to the second century C.E. Particularly valuable for its thorough treatment of the interaction between Judaism and Greek culture in Egypt.

Murray, William M., and Photios M Petsas. *Octavian's Campsite Memorial for the Actian War in Transactions of the American Philosophical Society.* Vol. 79, part 4. Philadelphia: American Philosophical Society, 1989. Lucid and detailed analysis of the archaeological evidence for the monument built by Augustus to commemorate the Battle of Actium.

Pomeroy, Sarah B. *Women in Hellenistic Egypt: From Alexander to Cleopatra.* 2nd ed. Detroit: Wayne State University Press, 1990. The author uses papyrological evidence to reconstruct the social and economic life of Greek women in Ptolemaic Egypt. She argues that activist queens like Cleopatra VII inspired the relative freedom illustrated by the lives of these women.

Richardson, Peter. *Herod: King of the Jews and Friend of the Romans.* Columbia, S.C.: University of South Carolina Press, 1996. Detailed biography of Herod, with particular attention to his relations to Rome.

Roller, Duane W. *The World of Juba II and Kleopatra Selene: Royal Scholarship On Rome's African Frontier.* London: Routledge, 2003. Pioneering reconstruction of the history and culture of Mauretania in the late first century B.C.E. and early first century C.E.

Royster, Francesca T. *Becoming Cleopatra: The Shifting Image of an Icon.* New York: Palgrave Macmillan, 2003. Postmodern study of the image of Cleopatra in twentieth-century-American popular culture. Particularly valuable for its analysis of the significance of Cleopatra as a symbol in African American cinema.

Sly, Dorothy. *Philo's Alexandria.* London: Routledge, 1996. Analysis of the representation of Alexandria in the works of the first-century C.E. Jewish philosopher Philo.

Solmsen, Friedrich. *Isis among the Greeks and Romans.* Cambridge, MA: Harvard University Press, 1979. Study of the transformation of Isis into an essentially Greek goddess outside Egypt.

Southern, Pat. *Augustus.* London: Routledge, 1998. Detailed political biography of the emperor Augustus based on the most recent scholarship.

————. *Cleopatra.* Charleston, S.C.: Tempus Publishing, 1999. Political biography of Cleopatra VII, with particular emphasis on her relations with Rome.

Stambaugh, John E. *Sarapis under the Early Ptolemies.* Leiden: Brill, 1972. Lucid account of the origin and early history of the cult of Sarapis. The author demonstrates that the spread of Sarapis outside Egypt was not promoted by the Ptolemies.

Thompson, Dorothy J. *Memphis Under the Ptolemies.* Princeton: Princeton University Press, 1988. A remarkable study of the ancient Egyptian capital. The author uses Greek and Egyptian papyri to reconstruct in detail the social and cultural life of the second city of Ptolemaic Egypt.

Volkmann, Hans. *Cleopatra: A Study in Politics and Propaganda.* Translated by T. J. Cadoux. New York: Sagamore Press, 1958. Standard scholarly biography of Cleopatra by a leading historian of Ptolemaic Egypt.

Walker, Susan, and Sally-Ann Ashton. *Cleopatra Reassessed.* The British Museum, 2003. Important collection of revisionist essays by leading scholars dealing with various aspects of Cleopatra's reign and its legacy.

————. *Cleopatra.* Bristol Classical Press, 2006. Brief introduction to the literary and artistic tradition concerning Cleopatra from antiquity to the present.

Walker, Susan, and Peter Higgs, eds. *Cleopatra of Egypt: From History to Myth.* Princeton: Princeton University Press, 2001. Lavishly illustrated catalogue of a major exhibition of representations of Cleopatra VII in European art. The volume includes a valuable series of essays on the image of Cleopatra from antiquity to the present.

Weigall, Arthur. *The Life and Times of Cleopatra Queen of Egypt: A Study in the Origin of the Roman Empire.* London: Putnam's Sons, 1924. A landmark book by a major early-twentieth-century Egyptologist. This work was the first study to treat Cleopatra primarily as a political figure instead of as a sexual predator.

Whitehorne, John. *Cleopatras.* London: Routledge, 1994. A well-documented series of brief biographies of all the Ptolemaic queens named Cleopatra except Cleopatra VII.

Witt, R. E. *Isis in the Graeco-Roman World.* Ithaca: Cornell University Press, 1971. Detailed study of the cult of Isis in Greek and Roman culture. The author treats the cult of Isis more as a forerunner than as a rival to early Christianity.

Web Sites

The internet contains a multitude of sites related to ancient history. There are two excellent sites dealing with Ptolemaic Egypt.

The House of Ptolemy. A large well-organized site containing links both to the individual Ptolemaic rulers and to primary and secondary sources relevant to Ptolemaic history. http://www.houseofptolemy.org.

Cleopatra on the Web. A comprehensive and well-organized site devoted entirely to the history and legacy of Cleopatra. http://www.isidore-of-seville.com/cleopatra/index.html.

Films

Antony and Cleopatra: Passion for Power. A&E Home Video. New York, 2002 (100 minutes). A beautifully photographed film emphasizing the relationship between Cleopatra and Antony. It includes extensive commentary by leading contemporary Roman historians.

Cleopatra (special edition). Twentieth Century Fox Home Video. Beverly Hills (248 minutes). Digitally remastered version of the 1963 film, together with extensive documentary material on its production and promotion.

Cleopatra: Destiny's Queen. Biography. A&E Home Video. New York, 1994 (50 minutes). A video biography of Cleopatra VII. It contains excellent visuals of Egypt and interesting commentary by contemporary Roman historians and Egyptologists. Unfortunately, it is also marred by numerous factual errors in the narrative.

Cleopatra's Palace: In Search of a Legend. Discovery Communications, Inc. Silver Springs, MD, 1999 (50 minutes). A well-produced popular documentary on the underwater excavations in Alexandria harbor. The film contains interesting visuals about the discoveries made on the sunken island of Antirrhodos, but makes little effort to explain the nature of underwater archaeology, emphasizing instead the search for objects and the "palace of Cleopatra."

INDEX